Children
of the Self–
Absorbed

**A Grownup's Guide
to Getting Over
Narcissistic Parents**

Nina W. Brown, Ed.D., L.P.C.

New Harbinger Publications, Inc.

Publisher's Note

This publication is designed to provide accurate and authoritative information in regard to the subject matter covered. It is sold with the understanding that the publisher is not engaged in rendering psychological, financial, legal, or other professional services. If expert assistance or counseling is needed, the services of a competent professional should be sought.

Distributed in Canada by Raincoast Books

Copyright © 2001 by Nina W. Brown
New Harbinger Publications, Inc.
5674 Shattuck Avenue
Oakland, CA 94609

Cover design by Blue Designs
Edited by Carole Honeychurch
Text design by Tracy Marie Powell

Library of Congress Card Catalog Number: 00-134861

ISBN-10 1-57224-231-0
ISBN-13 978-1-57224-231-9

Printed in the United States of America

New Harbinger Publications' Web site address: www.newharbinger.com

09   08   07

20   19   18   17   16   15   14

This book is dedicated to my husband, Wilford, my daughters, Toni and Linda, and their husbands, Bruce and Chris, and to my son, Michael, and his wife, Jill. They are good parents.

Contents

Chapter 9

Building Humor and Creativity   **171**

✱ Hurtful Humor ✱ Your Best Defenses ✱ Healthy
Humor ✱ Creativity ✱ Building Your Creativity

Chapter 10

Wrap-up Thoughts   **193**

✱ Give Up Your Fantasy ✱ Accept Your
Limitations ✱ Protect Yourself ✱ Self-Exploration and
Assessment ✱ Developing Your Healthy
Narcissism ✱ Understand Your Parent ✱ Be Patient
with Yourself ✱ Celebrate Your Progress ✱ Final Words

References   **205**

Foreword

This book grew out of my search for understanding of my reactions to a colleague who aroused considerable frustration and anguish in practically everyone this person encountered. However, none of us talked to each other about it and I continued to engage in much self-examination, looking for my unresolved issues that could be making me react so strongly to this person. Nothing I could think of seemed to fit, so I continued to try to dissolve my resistance and defenses, all to no avail.

A meeting with colleagues started me on a more fruitful path. The meeting was on a professional concern, but I happened to make a comment that I went home and took two headache pills after a recent conversation with the distressing colleague. I was surprised to hear from every person at the meeting (about ten people) that they, too, had headaches or stomachaches every time they interacted with the person. Although we didn't spend much time recounting our reactions and experiences, I realized that part of the problem was the other person. That realization sent me to the literature, and what emerged was the description for the destructive narcissistic pattern. Everything fit, including the personal reactions I'd had with the colleague.

Researching causes and development of the destructive narcissistic pattern (DNP) led me to reflect about the effects on a child when either one or both parents had the pattern. As I continued to explore the research, I began to better understand some of my personal experiences and those that many of my students and clients had reported. Many of their adult reactions, behaviors, and attitudes could be a result of having one or more parents who had a destructive narcissistic pattern.

Out of these realizations and experiences emerged this book. But understanding was not enough. If what I'd learned was to truly be helpful, I needed to find a way not only to explain the destructive narcissistic pattern in ways that would be easy to understand, but to provide some personal growth strategies as well. What I wanted to do was to give people some resources for providing themselves with the parenting they needed but did not receive. This was my challenge and what follows is my attempt to provide some understanding and guidance.

Acknowledgments

There are many people who assist an author with publishing a book. My ideas emerged from reading about the experiences of some expert and wise clinicians, and from interacting with and learning from the institutes, workshops, and personal experiences of members of the American Group Psychotherapy Association and members of its affiliate, the Mid-Atlantic Group Psychotherapy Society. I want to especially thank George Max Saiger, M.D., who was encouraging when I had the audacity to suggest the subclinical category of a destructive narcissistic pattern.

This book would not have been possible without the help of the supportive people at New Harbinger. Thanks to Kristin Beck, the acquisitions editor, Gretchen Gold for publicity, Amy Shoup, the art director, who designed the cover and, most of all, to Carole Honeychuch, the very patient editor.

Chapter 1

Destructive Narcissistic Parents

Parents with a destructive narcissistic pattern will have behaviors and attitudes that are designed to preserve a self-image of perfection, entitlement, and superiority. For the child's entire life the parent-child relationship was reversed, and the child, even after attaining adulthood, is expected to:

- absorb parental projections

- accept blame and criticism

- automatically know what the parent wants or needs and give it to him/her

- admire the parent and give unlimited attention

- never offend the parent

- understand that he/she is inferior to the parent and not react to demeaning comments

- realize that the parent will always know what is best for the child.

Adult children of parents who have a destructive narcissistic pattern will continue to feel the impact of their parent's behavior and attitudes and continue to suffer reactions that are as perplexing to them as they are distressing.

The DNP Illustrated

Mark's story below helps illustrate what can happen when adult children try to interact with parents who have a destructive narcissistic pattern.

Mark

When Mark, a thirty-year-old banker, hung up the phone he couldn't help feeling very angry and hurt. The call was from his father's secretary telling him that Mark's father would be in town from Friday through Sunday and wanted Mark to have dinner with him on Friday. Mark felt stung and angry because his father had had his secretary call instead of picking up the phone himself. On top of that, even though it had been six months since they last had dinner together, his father expected Mark to change whatever plans he may have had to accommodate his dad. As a matter of fact, Mark did have plans for that evening and he was really looking forward to attending a performance with a friend.

Mark was also still upset that his father had been too busy to meet with him the last time he was in town and had only called Mark when he was ready to return home. Mark thought, "He ignores me for months and then expects me to drop everything and run to him whenever he beckons." Not only was Mark angry, but he also felt ambivalent. He wanted both to have dinner with his father and to tell him to go to hell.

Mark had many conflicting feelings, chief of which seemed to be hurt. There are many other examples of relationships and interactions with the destructive narcissistic parent. Susan's has to do with her mom.

Susan

Susan was a forty-five-year-old mother of two who managed a large corporate office. She and her husband were dressing to go to her parents' house for her mother's birthday party, and Susan was having trouble choosing an outfit. She had put on several different things, but discarded them all. Her husband became exasperated and told her to just pick something. He was a little confused and frustrated because generally Susan did not have trouble deciding on what to wear. It only seemed to happen when she had to go to her parents' house.

Finally, Susan was dressed and the family left for the party. The children were the first out of the car and Susan trailed last. By the time she reached the door, the rest of her family was inside and her mother stood in the entrance waiting for her. As soon as Susan said, "Happy birthday, Mother," her mother frowned and said, "My God, Susan, you look terrible. What on earth made you buy a dress like that? It makes you look like a hooker." Susan felt like she'd been hit with a brick and had to resist the urge to take off running.

The experiences of Mark and Susan can only capture a small part of the feelings experienced when interacting with a parent who has a destructive narcissistic pattern. So much of what this parent does can be minimized by outsiders and excused as isolated events.

Mark was angry and upset at the attitude of entitlement his father seems to have, along with an inability to appreciate the impact of his behavior and attitude on Mark. What might contribute to Mark's reactions without him even being aware of it, is Mark's father's unconscious assumption that Mark is an extension of him (the father) and thus available whenever he wanted Mark.

Susan couldn't decide what to wear because she was anticipating demeaning and disparaging remarks from her mother, treatment she'd come to expect. Her mother never commented on her positive accomplishments, she only berated Susan for perceived failings. The anticipated put-down made Susan dithering and indecisive before every visit.

Both Mark and Susan were reacting from a lifetime of interacting with their destructive narcissistic parents. As adults, even the most casual interaction with the parents can cause hurt, anger, and feelings of helplessness and impotence. No matter how these "adult children" try to fortify themselves, even anticipating interactions with the parent produces distress.

You May Have a Similar Parent

Do you:

- dread interactions with a parent

- find ways to avoid them

- become easily frustrated and angry almost every time you talk with them

- leave their presence angry and churned up most every time you see them

- wish that they would disappear or that you never had to see or interact with them ever again?

Does a parent:

- constantly criticize you

- blame you for their discomfort

- make you responsible for their physical and/or emotional well-being

- expect you to admire them and give them constant attention

- insist that everything be done their way

- feel that you should anticipate their needs and desires and fulfill them

- become easily offended

- ignore, minimize, or discount your feelings

- make demeaning comments about you

- devalue your work or ideas

- micromanage or try to overcontrol you

- blame you or others for their errors?

If you answered "yes" to most of the behaviors and attitudes in the two lists, you may be the adult child of a parent with a destructive narcissistic pattern (DNP). You may also want to compare your behaviors and attitudes against the lists to see if you have incorporated any and are acting on them.

How can you tell if one or both of your parents had a destructive narcissistic pattern? After all, even the most well-meaning parents were not perfect and made mistakes. Also, what you recall as an adult is influenced by the stage of childhood you were in when the event you're recalling took place. You could be "stuck" at that level of development when remembering the particular event, causing you to react more strongly than otherwise. And, you may be dealing with incomplete information and understanding. All of these conditions combine to suggest that you cannot totally rely on what you remember and your interpretation of those events to decide if one or both of your parents had a destructive narcissistic pattern.

Two Means to Identification of the DNP

We will use two means to identify parental destructive narcissism: your behaviors, attitudes, and feelings as an adult and a pattern of consistent behaviors and attitudes of your parents.

The first focus is on you as an adult, because your sense of "self," acceptance of self and others, ability to develop and maintain satisfying relationships, self-efficacy, self-confidence, and expectations of self and of others are all influenced by your perceptions of your childhood, parents, and family life. There are other influences that are important, like culture, personality, and genetics, but those listed may be basic and, because they are deep seated, may continue to impact your physical, emotional, psychological, and spiritual well-being.

Another reason for focusing on *you* is that much of this book presents suggestions and techniques to help you cope with your parents as they are now. You, as an adult, may still be responding to your parents as you did when you were a child, and you want to begin to respond to them as an adult. Actually, what you probably really want is to stop feeling the way you do when they trigger unwanted and unpleasant feelings, or to make them stop behaving and having the attitudes that hurt you. This book can help you change the way you feel, but almost nothing can help you to change someone else. The book also presents some ways to identify developmental areas where you may have been stuck in childhood and strategies to grow and develop in these areas.

A way you can closely examine the consistent behaviors and attitudes displayed by your parent(s) is by completing the scales in the following two chapters. The list of questions earlier in this chapter can also be a guide. What you're looking for is not only the way your parent(s) act toward you, but the behaviors and attitudes that seem to be an integral part of them and can be observed and felt in their other relationships. What you're trying to discover is if there is a *pattern of behavior that indicates destructive narcissism.*

Narcissism—Who Needs It?

Narcissism is commonly defined many ways. It's most often considered to be excessive self-love, when a person is self-absorbed in almost everything he or she does and says. This definition is certainly the basis for the diagnosis of pathological narcissism or for the narcissistic personality disorder. However, current thinking about narcissism has extended the definition to also describe self-love that is healthy, such as self-esteem. Narcissism is also considered by some to be a normal part of psychological growth and development, which expands our understanding of what is called "age-appropriate narcissism." "Age appropriate" simply means that the person has healthy narcissism for his/her age. An example would be the way a child understands everything in terms of self and is expected to be self-absorbed. The same behavior and attitude in an adult would not be age-appropriate, healthy narcissism.

Adults who do not have age-appropriate, healthy narcissism can exhibit other categories for narcissism such as:

- stable narcissism

- underdeveloped narcissism

- a destructive narcissistic pattern

- pathological narcissism.

Think of adult narcissism as existing on a continuum ranging from pathological (not healthy) to healthy. The other categories will fall along the continuum, with stable narcissism closest to healthy narcissism and the destructively narcissistic pattern closest to pathological narcissism. Adults need healthy narcissism to have strong self-esteem and in order to form and maintain meaningful relationships. Healthy narcissism is an ideal but achievable state. This book focuses on some strategies that can assist in building healthy narcissism or, at the very least, developing some aspect of any underdeveloped narcissism that may be lingering. In other words, I'll be helping you move toward the healthy side of the narcissist continuum and away from those patches of underdeveloped narcissism that may be keeping you stuck in old, childhood ways of reacting.

Healthy Adult Narcissism

It may be best to begin with a description of healthy adult narcissism. This description is based on Kohut's (1977) description of healthy adult narcissism in his book, *The Restoration of the Self*, and proposed stages of narcissism development related to age. Viewing narcissism in this way takes away a stigma of it being a "bad" thing to have.

Kohut described adults with healthy narcissism as:

- having empathy

- having a sense of humor

- being creative.

In my book on destructive narcissism (1998), it seemed appropriate to add:

- an ability to delay gratification

- assumption of responsibility to self and to others

- a capacity to develop and maintain meaningful and satisfying relationships

- a deep and broad range of emotional expressiveness

- firm and clear boundaries.

Empathy

Empathy is the ability to sense and feel what the other person is experiencing. It's not sympathy or simply understanding, but being able to put yourself in the other person's shoes and feel what they would feel in a specific situation. Often, what the other person is feeling is discomfort of some kind, and we generally tend to shy away from discomfort or intense emotions. The ability to open yourself up and allow yourself to feel the discomfort and/or intense emotions experienced by another person should be accompanied with strong boundaries so that you do not get overwhelmed or incorporated into the emotions. In other words, you have to be able to feel but also be able to pull yourself back from the feelings, accepting that these are the other person's feelings, not yours.

Many people can be sympathetic, but that's really not the same as empathy. You can feel for the other person, be sorry that they are experiencing discomfort, but still have some detachment so that you do not end up feeling as they do. Some may even understand how the person feels and why they feel as they do without having either sympathy or empathy. Their feelings are even more detached.

A Sense of Humor

Having a sense of humor is uplifting. The ability to laugh is healthy and has been shown to be beneficial to your physical well-being. Being able to see absurdities, to laugh at yourself, and to see humor in a play on words call for a high level of understanding, acceptance, intelligence, and maturity. Humor is complicated, but an adult sense of humor is characterized by a lack of meanness, a willingness to accept one's imperfections, and an ability to see the absurdity of life.

The book, *Mind/Body Health* (Hafen et al. 1996), has an entire chapter describing the physical and psychological benefits of humor. Their emphasis is on research findings that support the positive and even healing benefits of humor. Humor has been shown to:

- dissipate stress

- provide pain relief

- decrease accidents on the job

- enhance self-esteem

- encourage a broad perspective on life

- strengthen the immune system

- promote creativity

- improve negotiating and decision-making skills

- help maintain a sense of emotional balance

- improve performance

- give a sense of power

- promote coping skills

- diminish fear

- calm anger

- relieve depression.

There are many physical and psychological benefits for being able to laugh and see humor in life situations.

Creativity

Creativity, in adults, can be termed as inventiveness and imagination in producing something original. The operative idea is to produce something that did not exist before. You can be creative in thinking up solutions to problems, producing new objects, taste sensations, processes, and so on. The range for creativity is broad and deep.

Why is creativity considered to be a characteristic of healthy narcissism? After all, children, whose narcissism is naturally underdeveloped, can be very creative. However, kids are somewhat limited in what they are able to create, whereas adults with healthy narcissism have unlimited capacity for creativity and, indeed, bring this capacity to many different aspects of their lives. Their attitudes are different in that they look for novel, more effective and efficient ways of doing almost everything.

For example, the parent who finds ways of providing nourishing and tasteful meals on a regular basis, day after day, year in and year out, would not generally be perceived as creative—but they are. It takes thought, effort, and originality to be able to accomplish this task. Just apply the same principle to other life situations and you expand your understanding of creativity.

Those who are immature or who have underdeveloped narcissism do not seek out original, inventive solutions or ways to accomplish tasks. They tend to stick with what they are familiar with instead of being open to examining situations to come up with more creative ways to perform or be.

The creative adult is open, flexible, and finds satisfaction in seeking new and original ways to make life better. While it's easy to see what's creative in works such as art, music, drama, dance, and literature, a little thought allows other forms of creativity to be appreciated.

Delaying Gratification

A definite sign of mature, healthy narcissism is the ability to delay gratification. Curbing impatience, containing anxiety, and being able to appropriately substitute satisfying others' needs instead of your own are also a part of healthy narcissism. The adult with healthy narcissism understands and is willing to accept that sometimes their needs cannot be immediately satisfied and are willing to wait. They understand that they can meet their own needs later, and don't have to panic if it doesn't happen right away. They are able to tolerate some discomfort and feel confident that the situation is temporary and not chronic.

Delaying gratification also points out the ability of the person to accept that someone else's needs may be of more importance at that moment. For example, the ability to delay gratification allows parents to give children the nurturing that they need, even when it calls for extensive sacrifice on the part of parents. They are willing to allow the children's gratification to take precedence over their needs.

Assumption of Responsibility

When you assume responsibility for yourself you accept that you're not perfect and don't blame others for your imperfections. One of the prominent characteristics of the destructive narcissist is their tendency to off-load blame. They can never accept that they were at fault, did something wrong, or made a mistake. It's always someone else's fault that they goofed. The adult with healthy narcissism doesn't try to wiggle out of their responsibility for what happened. They may not like having to accept that they made a mistake, but they don't blame others when they do.

Assumption of responsibility also means taking responsibility for your actions and decisions, or for your lack of both. It's true that life circumstances often dictate what alternatives people have, but the responsible adult accepts that they have ultimate responsibility for what they did and what they do.

Meaningful Relationships

The ability to develop and maintain meaningful relationships is a characteristic of mature people and healthy narcissism. It is our relationships that help reduce loneliness and alienation and that give meaning to our lives. Having satisfying relationships is very important for our emotional and psychological health.

The destructive narcissist will often have difficulty in developing and maintaining meaningful relationships. They will have numerous partners, marry and divorce often, and flit from person to person in search of the perfect friend. They choose partners and friends on the basis of what that person can do for them, especially in terms of status. Some people with a DNP only have friends that they consider to be superior in status.

These are very lonely and empty people. They seem to have no core and substitute activity for relationships. They may seem to give a lot to their relationships, but on closer examination it becomes clear that they aren't genuinely responsive to others and are intensely self-focused.

The old story about an artist at a party illustrates some of what I mean. The artist was talking with an acquaintance and the acquaintance was struck with the fact that the whole conversation was all about the artist. What he did, what he thought, who he knew, and on and on. After a while the artist said, "Enough about me. Let's talk about you. Have you seen my exhibit at the downtown gallery?" No matter what they seem to be talking about, self-absorbed people are really talking about themselves.

It's not easy for anyone to initiate, develop, and maintain satisfying relationships. Conflicts emerge, you become disappointed with each other or yourself, and problems can seem constant. However, many people care enough about each other to persevere in the face of these difficult circumstances. The relationship is important enough to try and work through the difficulties. The payoffs are intimacy, trust, connections, and meaningfulness. The destructive narcissist lacks these and constantly seeks to get them by moving from person to person. Unable to truly invest in any one relationship, it's not unusual to find that they marry and divorce three or more times, or have numerous partners.

Range of Emotions

Adults with healthy narcissism not only has a wide range of emotions, they are also able to experience intense positive and negative emotions. On the other hand, the destructive narcissist has a restricted range of emotions and almost all of those have the depth of a line.

Research (Hafen et al. 1998) has shown that emotions affect health. Negative emotions have a negative effect on health, and positive emotions have a positive effect. This is not to say that one should ignore reality and focus only on the positive. The psychologically healthy person does not ignore reality. However, they do try to remember the positive while dealing constructively with the negative.

How does this relate to emotional expressivity? There is considerable research illustrating the negative effects of anger on people's physical and psychological well-being. Indeed, some very serious illnesses are shown to have strong connections with some negative emotions (like heart disease and hostility). On the other hand, people who are happy tend also to be in better or good health.

The destructive narcissist will be able to use the correct words for emotions, but will not have the feelings associated with the words. For example, they will use the words "happy" and "joy" correctly but will not be able to feel happiness or joy. If you listen carefully, what you will hear them express most often is anger, despair, and fear. They don't seem to be able to express milder forms of these emotions, like annoyance, sadness, or apprehension. They are unable to speak of more positive emotions with any feeling. Because positive emotions are generally unavailable to them, their words about them have a hollow sound.

The person with healthy adult narcissism is able to feel and express a broad range and variety of emotions. By "range" I mean levels of emotions, from mild to intense. The person with healthy narcissism can feel a wide variety of emotions in a variety of ways. They are open and flexible emotionally.

Firm and Clear Boundaries

A major psychological developmental task that everyone must achieve is to separate and individuate. That means that you need to have an understanding and acceptance of where you end and others begin. This understanding is one way to think of boundaries. Not only do you understand where you end and another begins, but you can maintain that separation with words and action. The person who is incomplete in some part of separating and individuating can overstep the set limits or boundaries without even knowing what they're doing. They don't see the boundary because they can't recognize where they end and you begin.

Maintaining boundaries can be difficult since bringing to someone's attention that they are violating your boundaries can be upsetting to them. There are social conventions that would term this "rude" under certain conditions. For example, if someone walks into your office without knocking and you point that out to them, they can become offended and perceive you as hostile and rude. All you were really doing was pointing out to them that they did not observe a boundary that is important to you.

The adult with healthy narcissism will have firm and clear boundaries. They respect other's boundaries and insist that their boundaries be respected by others. They are not rude or aloof, just aware of who they are and willing to give the same respect to others. The destructive narcissist, on the other hand, will often violate boundaries. This can be very frustrating, as they're usually unaware of their violations and can get very confused and upset when you mention them. This is even worse with parents, where we often walk a thin line between maintaining our boundaries and showing proper respect for them.

Stable Narcissism

Kohut (1977) suggests that adults who have primarily healthy narcissism but may lag in some development have "stable narcissism." There is still room for growth, although the person may exhibit some milder versions of behaviors and attitudes that are not quite as developed as they could be.

For example, the person who can be empathic with many but has difficulty being empathic with some could be someone with stable narcissism in that area. Personal vanity can be stable narcissism as long as it is not carried to extremes. Other examples could be:

- use of moderate attention-getting strategies without feeling devastated if they don't work

- wanting respect and recognition for accomplishments but not demanding admiration

- wishing their children would take their advice but not rejecting them when they do not

- becoming aware and accepting of differences among people

- not expecting others to read their minds

- understanding their limitations for feeling and expressing emotions

- not expecting or wanting others to envy them.

Pathological Narcissism

Even experienced clinicians have difficulty diagnosing narcissistic personality disorder or pathological narcissism at first. It seems that it takes a period of contact with the person before the pathology emerges. Further, the diagnosis depends a great deal on the reactions of the therapist to the person.

This difficulty occurs because the pathological narcissist is usually very adept at disguising their behaviors and attitudes. It's mainly the person's attitudes that lead to the label, and attitudes can be concealed for a very long time. What generally happens is that the therapist begins to be aware that he/she

- has a profound wish that the person would not return or would go to another therapist

- feels increasingly incompetent and unable to please or satisfy the person

- is frustrated and angry after sessions with the person

- begins to question his/her competence, knowledge, and skills.

The Destructive Narcissistic Pattern

A destructive narcissistic pattern is a constellation of behaviors and attitudes for an individual that:

- produces considerable and constant frustration for others who have to interact with them on a regular basis

- significantly impacts the person's ability to develop and maintain satisfying relationships

- constitutes many of the same psychological developmental delays as do those who have more pathological narcissism

- are characterized by unrealistic expectations that others exist for their personal benefit.

It's almost impossible for a therapist or anyone else to identify these aspects in someone as characteristic of DNP until they've spent some time with the person. It is only over time and with consensual validation by other people who've experienced similar things with the person that one can arrive at the conclusion that the person is indeed a destructive narcissist. If others do not have the same perceptions or problems, then you need to do more self-examination to determine if your behaviors and attitudes are producing the reactions you're experiencing.

You may be convinced by this time that one or more of your parents fits the description for having a destructive narcissistic pattern. However, what is described in chapter 1 is the general framework for beginning to understand the impact of destructive narcissism but does not give enough information to make a decision about your parent(s). Further, old hurts and resentments may be clouding your perceptions of your parent(s). It would be helpful if you could try and stay somewhat objective until you work through the material in chapters 2 and 3.

The material in chapter 2 describes some specific behaviors and attitudes that will help you determine if your parent fits the destructive narcissistic pattern. Suggestions are also provided for obtaining outside checks of your perceptions. Chapter 3 begins to turn the focus on you by having you reflect on the extent to which parental self-absorbed behaviors and attitudes continue to impact your current relationships, meaning of life, and overall well-being.

Chapter 2

Does Your Parent Have a Destructive Narcissistic Pattern (DNP)?

One of the most difficult jobs, if not the most difficult one, is being a parent. It's an extremely intensive, draining, and unrelenting task for which most people receive little preparation. The lucky ones get support and needed information, but many people aren't that lucky. Yet many parents, in spite of ignorance, lack of preparation, and high probability for error, manage to rear their children to be good, emotionally stable citizens. Most parents do the very best they can, although what they can do may not be very good. It's important to remember this as you read about parental destructive narcissism and get back in touch with old hurts and resentments. Even if your parents turn out to have a DNP, they behaved the best they could under the circumstances.

What I present here is not intended to condemn parents with destructive narcissism. What I'd like to do is to describe and explain what behaviors, attitudes, and feelings these parents may have had that led them to do or say things, or demand things from the child that were:

- inappropriate for the child's stage of development

- wounding

- stifling to the child's emotional development

- disruptive to the child's psychological growth.

I'm hoping that some understanding of these topics will lead to increased self-understanding, growth, development, and greater self-esteem and self-acceptance. These are the inner states that can help you, as an adult, better cope with your parents. Your parents will not be able to as easily trigger emotions and old parental messages, which can enable you to interact with them on an adult basis instead of continuing to respond as you did as a child.

The Child as Parent

Children who have to assume a parent's role often have done so from a very early age and don't know any other way of being. They are so conditioned that they assume their experience is universal. Even when they become aware of other ways of being and behaving, they are frequently unable to break away from this early conditioning. They are the "parentified child."

The child who has to take care of their parent(s) was termed "parentified" by researchers in the 70s and 80s (Boszormenyi-Nagy and Framo [1985]; Minuchin [1974]). The child behaves as a parent should in ensuring that the parent's emotional and sometimes physical needs are met, even though it's generally understood to be the parent's responsibility to meet the child's needs and take care of him/her.

There are numerous situations that can result in a "parentified child," such as:

- a depressed parent

- a chronically ill parent

- a parent who is seriously emotionally disturbed
- the death of one parent
- a parent's grieving
- a parent's inability to find employment
- a seriously ill sibling or other close relative
- a destructive narcissistic pattern.

The common thread that runs through all of these situations is that the parent is not available to meet the child's needs and has become so needy that the child is forced to assume the parent's role.

Do you recall your parent saying any of the following, or something similar?

- "Why can't you do something to make me feel good?"
- "_____ (usually a sibling) saw that I was upset, but you continued to play. You're so selfish."
- "I can't feel like a good mother (or father) when you do that."
- "I need you to take care of me. I love you when you want me to feel good."
- "I feel like such a failure when you're so selfish."

If you constantly heard comments like these, you could be a parentified child.

Most parents do not consciously set out to reverse roles. Indeed, if challenged, they would maintain that they *are* being parents, and doing so quite well, under the circumstances. The reversal that takes place is subtle and unconscious, which keeps the parentification hidden. Further, some behaviors like micromanaging and overcontrolling can appear to be a parental function when, in reality, the behavior is only another way of getting the child to meet the parent's needs. This can be especially true for parents who have a destructive narcissistic pattern. An example is when a parent has to approve of everything the child wears all the time. The child is never allowed to express or exhibit any personal preference about their clothes. If the parent does not like a particular color or style, then the child is simply not permitted to wear it. The parent's need is to have other people admire how well they have dressed their child, or to receive admiration for their great taste. The focus must be on the parent, and the child's wishes are ignored.

The Effects of Parentification

A parent with a DNP does not, or cannot, respond to the child's needs. They are not at a level where they are able to:

- nurture

- respond empathically

- put the child's needs ahead of their own

- appreciate the child as a separate individual

- be patient when the child is demanding

- give unconditional positive regard to the child

- allow the child to be less than perfect without considerable disapproval

- tune in to the emotional life and needs of the child.

They simply aren't emotionally and psychologically available for the child. In addition to being unavailable, the child is expected to meet the parent's needs for:

- attention

- admiration

- entitlement

- emotional satisfaction.

The child constantly receives messages about what they are supposed to be or do for the parent. When the child becomes an adult, the messages and expectations are so internalized that the child tends to respond to others in the same way they responded (and continue to respond) to their parent(s). Either they cater to others and find themselves resenting it, or they rebel and become unresponsive when their old parental messages are triggered.

Identifying a Parental DNP

The impact of parental attitudes and behaviors on you is one source for identifying a parental DNP. Another source of information is the consistent behavior of the parent(s) over time. We'll use both sources to help determine if your parent(s) had a destructive narcissistic pattern. As you read the examples, reflect on your behaviors, attitudes, and feelings to see if you're doing some of the same things your parents did and/or still do. Also remember that you are looking for any areas of underdeveloped narcissism in yourself (places where you got stuck in childhood) so that you can begin to grow in those areas. You don't have to stay stuck in old patterns and you certainly don't have to end up with your own destructive narcissistic pattern.

Consider the following description and discussion of behaviors and attitudes that indicate a destructive narcissistic pattern. There are nine categories to examine:

- attention needs

- admiration needs

- having to be considered unique and special

- lack of empathy

- extensions of self

- grandiosity

- shallow emotions

- exploitation of others

- emotional abusiveness.

The behaviors and attitudes described in each category are simply examples and don't necessarily include all the possible behaviors and attitudes in that category. As you read through each one, try to rate the extent to which your parent(s) exhibited them. The scale used will be:

5 – Always or almost always

4 – Frequently

3 – Sometimes

2 – Seldom

1 – Never, or almost never

Having a high score in one or two categories doesn't necessarily indicate a destructive narcissistic pattern, but having a high score in five or more categories definitely could. The designation is tentative at this point because there are still two other sets of indicators needed—validation from others and your persistent reactions.

Consensual Validation and Persistent Reactions

It's important to determine if others experience your parent(s) in the same way as you do before making a decision about their potential. Others do not have to answer all the items for validation, but you would want to check out some parental behaviors and attitudes to see if others perceive them as you do. Other people close to your parent(s) such as siblings, aunts, uncles, grandparents, and close friends can serve as sources. Your siblings are especially valuable, because others not as close will not necessarily have the same perceptions, experiences, or reactions that you do, but your siblings have perceptions and reactions similar to yours.

Validation is not a formal process and it can certainly be done in a nonsystematic way. When the opportunity arises, you could begin by telling the person that it seems to you that your parent does _____ . Fill in the blank with something like:

- turns every conversation to him or herself

- ignores the impact of their comments on you

- constantly criticizes or berates you

- seem to focus on blaming rather than accepting responsibility

- expects you to jump at their every whim.

Ask the person if they notice the same thing, or if the perception is uniquely yours. If the parent has a DNP, then it's likely that the person will either agree that your perception is what he/she too experiences, or that there is something else about the parent that is frustrating to him/her. If you discover that your experience is limited to you, then that may be a signal that you need to do more self-examination to determine if your parent's criticisms have some basis in fact.

The other crucial source of information will be your usual and persistent reactions to the parent(s). If you have consistent reactions over years to behaviors and attitudes of your parent, particularly if you've really tried to react differently and can't, then you may very well be reacting to the behaviors and attitudes of the destructive narcissistic pattern. Protective and coping strategies for these reactions will be discussed in more detail in chapters 4 and 5.

Preparation for Identifying

Sit in silence for a moment. Reflect on the parent you think may have a DNP. Try to recall some behaviors and attitudes they exhibited through the years. Do not judge or evaluate the behaviors or attitudes, just let them emerge. As difficult as it may be, try to detach your emotional reaction. What you're trying to do at this point is to determine if what you think you remember and how you presently experience your parent are reflective of parental destructive narcissism. You cannot help but have some emotional reactions as you remember painful situations and events, but you'll get more out of the exercise if you avoid becoming mired in them.

Rate the extent to which the parent generally, over the years, behaved as described or had the designated attitude. If you are rating both parents, rate them separately, using the rating system described before (rating 1 through 5). The total rating for each category indicates how many behaviors and attitudes associated with the category the parent exhibits, and how strongly they are manifested.

Attention Needs

Following are some behaviors and attitudes that suggest a need for attention. Rate your parent(s) on each item.

1. Brags

2. Has tantrums

3. Is loud and boisterous

4. Sulks

5. Has lots of complaints

6. Has an attitude of, "Anything you can do, I can do better."

7. Engages in one-upmanship

8. Continually teases others

9. Engages in seductive behaviors

10. Waits to be coaxed

The person with considerable attention needs becomes uncomfortable when the spotlight is turned to someone else, even to their child. This parent can bask in their child's accomplishments only when he/she, the parent, is receiving the credit. It's as if they are directly responsible for the child's accomplishment.

Whenever the spotlight turns from this parent, he/she does or says something to get it back. For example, let's suppose that you and your parent are at an awards event where you're receiving an award. People are coming up to congratulate you when, suddenly, your parent begins regaling the crowd in a loud voice about how you couldn't ride a bicycle until you were ten. This behavior immediately gets the spotlight off of you and on the parent. It has the further result of embarrassing you so much that you want to leave—and leaving means that you no longer get any attention. If you protest to the parent about the behavior, he/she probably counters by accusing you of being oversensitive.

The parent's attention-seeking behaviors are constant and not limited to immediate family. It doesn't seem to matter who is present or what's going on—when attention is focused on others, this person will inevitably do or say something to attract attention. They seem to find many reasons to engage in one-upmanship and "anything you can do, I can do better" and never pass up an opportunity to do so. They will go to great lengths, even going into considerable debt to buy goods and services that meet their need for attention.

Admiration Needs

Rate your parent(s) on each of the following:

1. Fishes for compliments and/or approval

2. Does it all; is a "superman" or "superwoman"

3. Isn't satisfied unless they have the "biggest" or "best"

4. Becomes overextended to get unneeded goods and services

5. Spends money to impress others

6. Neglects family to do things to impress others

7. Flaunts their possessions

8. Is vain

9. Gloats when he/she "wins"

10. Seeks status

11. Expects others to show gratitude

12. Expects you to constantly admire him/her

What lies beneath excessive admiration needs is the desire that others be envious. Envy is not only the desire to have what the other person has, it also incorporates resentment toward that person, and the feeling that the envious person is more worthy and should have whatever the envied person has.

Another characteristic seems to be the inability to be modest or quiet about accomplishments or possessions. There is an exhibitionistic quality that is revealed by their bragging, boasting, flaunting, or gloating. In short, these folks just aren't shy about letting you know what they've done or what they have. They'll go to extremes to have others look and speak admiringly of them.

These are also the status seekers. They value those they consider to be superior in status, seek to imitate them, and to bask in their reflected glory. They can then be admired for being like, or close to, the person of superior status. You'll notice that the person with admiration-seeking needs wants only to be associated with those they consider to be superior in status. Many of their choices for friends, social clubs, church, schools, and activities are based on who the participants are and/or the status the organization has.

Parents with a destructive narcissistic pattern not only seek admiration for what they do or have, they seek admiration from their children and about their children. The child seems to be valued for the admiration brought to the parent for what the child is or does. This aspect is explored more fully in the section called "Extensions of Self." The other part, expectations of admiration from the child, is seen in parental demands for gratitude and the constant need of compliments from the child.

The Need to Be Unique and Special

Rate the extent to which your parent(s) exhibit the following:

1. Does not obey minor laws (for example, not parking in a fire lane or other "no parking" zone)

2. Becomes angry when ignored or overlooked in some way

3. Tries to impress others with gifts, contributions, etc.

4. Does not wait their turn

5. Expects to be taken care of before others (for example, being seated in a restaurant)

6. Expects to receive "more" (attention, service, etc.) than others

7. Does not expect to be penalized for failure to follow directions, meet deadlines, or conform to guidelines

8. Tries to find ways around rules and laws

9. Belongs to exclusive clubs or organizations

10. Feels that what they have to say is more important than what anyone else can offer (frequently interrupts others)

Everyone can appreciate feeling unique and special from time to time. Indeed, one of the reasons we fall in love or become attracted to someone is their ability to make us feel that way. However, the person who has an excessive need to feel unique and special expects *everyone* to make them feel that way all of the time. They can be easily displeased or even angered when others do not act to make them feel unique and special.

This expectation can also apply to their children. The child is supposed to do and say things that make the parent feel unique and special, and it's up to the child to figure out what will make the parent feel that way. The child learns by trial and error what to say and do that will please the parent. The child who does not tune in to this parental demand or expectation will likely find that they are more often criticized, disparaged, and devalued than the sibling who meets the unspoken expectation.

When the child internalizes the expectations that their parent's needs are to be anticipated and met without them having to verbalize or make them known, it gives all the responsibility of meeting the parent's needs to the child. This internalized responsibility is then extended to others, and the child begins to judge their self-worth by the extent to which they can meet these expectations. Others may not even have these expectations, but because neither is talking about the dynamic, the child assumes that they are supposed to meet these unspoken needs just as they did with the parent. What's more, this isn't even a conscious act for the child. This unconscious sense of responsibility for others' welfare can and does persist into adulthood.

A Lack of Empathy

Did, or does, your parent do the following? Rate each item.

1. Call you "touchy" or "oversensitive" when you object to their slighting or disparaging comments about you

2. Ignore your feelings

3. Tell you that you "ought" or "should" not feel a particular feeling

4. Diminish the importance of a feeling you expressed

5. Fail to listen to you

6. Change the topic when you're talking about something that has emotional intensity for you

7. Do or say something to distract you from an intense feeling

8. Make criticizing or devaluing comments about you when you express emotions

9. Tell you how you "brought it on yourself" if you express a negative feeling

10. Is more interested in their concerns than in yours

Destructive narcissistic parents are focused more on personal needs than the child's needs. They either are unable to be empathic with the child or choose not to be empathic. One characteristic of healthy adult narcissism is empathy, but if the parent has not developed this aspect of self, they cannot be empathic with the child.

Being empathic doesn't necessarily mean being approving. It means that you're able to sense the inner world of the other person and feel what they're feeling without losing your sense of self. You can really feel the other person's experience but can also withdraw from the feeling when you decide to, not becoming enmeshed or overwhelmed.

Emotionally susceptible people, on the other hand, are prone to getting caught up in others' emotions without the ability to pull away. They don't have strong emotional boundaries and can easily be taken over with others' emotions. They start out by trying to empathize but do not have the firm understanding of where they end and others begin. This leads to their assuming the emotions of the other person—whether they want to or not.

When you grow up with a destructive narcissistic parent, you may find yourself exhibiting one of two responses, neither of which is empathy. You may be emotionally susceptible and "catch" others' emotions, becoming enmeshed or overwhelmed, or you shut yourself away from others' emotions, fearing enmeshment or engulfment because that is what happened with the parent.

Extensions of Self

Two major developmental tasks are separation and individuation. These are the psychological tasks of understanding our physical, emotional, and psychological boundaries—where we stop and others begin. Children who aren't allowed to successfully complete separation and individuation from the major caretaker, can end up with an incomplete understanding of what is "self" (a part of them and under their control) and what is not self (not under their control). This is what is meant by "extensions of self": The person does not fully comprehend where they (self) stop and where others begin.

Rate the extent to which your parent does the following:

1. Expects you to immediately drop what you're doing and attend to them

2. Uses your possessions without first asking permission

3. Enters your room without knocking and asking for permission

4. Gets angry when you do not act as they tell you to

5. Wants to control what you do and say

6. Is offended if you have an opinion or value that is different from theirs

7. Gave you their name (i.e., "junior")

8. Tries to micromanage you

9. Forces you to accept unwanted touching, caresses, kisses

10. Makes you feel helpless, stupid, or inept when you don't rely on them to tell you what to do and how to do it

The parent who failed to successfully complete separation and individuation will be unable to perceive their child as a completely separate individual and will consider them to be an extension of him or herself. This perception leads to:

• boundary violations

• overcontrolling behavior

• micromanaging

• feelings of resentment if the child rebels.

This need to control and manage is vastly different from providing guidance. Guidance carries the assumption that the other person is free to make some choices—they are not compelled to follow the guidance. However, in the controlling nature of extensions of self, there is no leeway for making a choice. The child is expected to feel compelled to accept the parent's dictates. The consequence for not accepting them or exercising any free will can be severe.

Grandiosity

Grandiosity involves an inflated perception of self that carries the implication of false pretensions. In other words, the person constantly exaggerates and puffs up their accomplishments, giving the impression that they just might not be telling the whole truth about their accomplishments. Affectation, which is a show of something designed to impress others, often shows up with grandiosity. Underneath the grandiosity can be a secret fear of inadequacy—a suggestion that the person firmly denies to others and self. The grandiose person doesn't allow any hint of personal inadequacy to become conscious. As far as they're concerned, they are grander, more competent, more worthy and deserving than anyone else. They can perform superhuman feats, making them superior to others.

You may not understand your parent's grandiosity by looking directly at their behavior, but you'll be able to spot it by looking at your reactions to their behavior. In some ways, it can be difficult to completely separate grandiosity from need for attention and admiration. The grandiose person does demand attention and admiration, but apart from that, there can also be an overly grand attitude. It may be that you only become aware of their grandiosity when you reflect on what was done or said, together with your reaction to it.

Rate the extent to which your parent does the following:

1. Is unable to laugh at him/herself

2. Is easily offended at any hint that they are wrong or mistaken

3. Knows what is "best" for you

4. Is intensely wounded by even the mildest disagreement with their opinions or suggestions

5. Is arrogant

6. Expects to win

7. Consider that they are essential for your survival

8. Is flamboyant

9. Boasts

10. Considers others as inferior (appearance, ability, status, money, etc.)

Whatever the nature of the grandiosity this parent will be wounded (narcissistically wounded) by any indication that you do not consider them to be as important, essential, or grand as they perceive themselves to be. (A narcissistic wound is an insult or hurt to the essential self.) Even if you mildly disagree with their opinion about something of little importance, they can be seriously hurt, as they perceive this as a rejection of their essential self. They have to scrupulously maintain their perceptions that they are:

- in control of everything

- stupendous

- fabulous

- magnificent

- essential

- superior

- the center of the universe.

Shallow Emotions

Destructive narcissists are likely to have shallow emotions, except for anger and fear. Their emotions seem no deeper than a dewdrop. This is one reason why they cannot empathize. They do not know what it is to truly experience:

- happiness

- joy

- sadness

- despair

- shame

- guilt

- love.

Because they don't experience these emotions, they cannot really understand what you or anyone else is experiencing.

They do seem to be able to talk about emotions as though they can experience them, but a closer look is likely to show that the feelings do not accompany the expression. For example, if you were to tell the parent with a DNP that you were sad, they would probably respond with words that seemed to be understanding of your feeling. However, the next statement or expression would veer off the subject, would be about them or criticism of you.

Or let's take a situation where they tell you they are sad, and you respond empathically or with understanding. As you continue to talk, you realize that what they seem to be expressing and feeling is anger—not sadness. Or, as soon as you are hooked, they change the subject and you're left still under the effects of their real feeling, the anger. You are churned up, tense, uncomfortable, and don't know how you got that way nor how to let it go.

These are the parents who manage to "throw rain on your parade." When you are happy, triumphant, or joyful, they can make a comment that introduces a little gloom, usually some disparaging remark about you. You either ignore it, protest, or allow it to lessen your joy. They can easily get to you. Why do they rain on your parade? One reason is that they don't understand what you're feeling, as they cannot access these feelings within themselves. They pretend to have them, but you can tell, with some practice, that it's a pretense and not a real feeling.

Entitlement

The destructive narcissist generally has a well-developed entitlement attitude, which can drive nearly anyone crazy. A person with an entitlement attitude generally carries the assumption that they are more important than others, more deserving, and therefore should receive:

- more attention

- special consideration

- choice goods and services

- deference.

Further, they shouldn't have to:

- abide by rules, regulations, or laws

- be considerate of others

- wait around

- stand in line

- defer to others

- defer gratification.

This entitlement attitude in parents with destructive narcissism could result in some of the following behaviors. Rate the extent to which your parent exhibits these.

1. Gives orders and expects immediate obedience

2. Expects you to always defer to them

3. Makes negative or demeaning comments and expects you to accept them without protest

4. Interrupts you to do something for them, even if you're busy

5. Sends you on their personal errands

6. Assumes that their wants and needs take priority over yours

7. Expects lavish gifts

8. Becomes irate when you're not effusive in expressing gratitude or thanks

9. Takes the best of everything

10. Insists that things be done their way

Someone with a heightened entitlement attitude can easily make others feel that they are being judged and found to be flawed. This unconscious assumption that others exist only to serve the entitled person's needs produces rage and fury in others. Thwarting the person who has this attitude produces rage in them. It seems that whatever you do, either you wind up angry or they do.

Exploiting Others

Rate the extent to which your parent exhibits the following behaviors.

1. Lies

2. Exaggerates

3. Distorts

4. Makes misleading statements

5. Expects favors from you but doesn't return them

6. Manipulates you

7. Uses emotional blackmail

8. Makes others emotionally dependent on them

In some ways, exploitation of others is connected to an entitlement attitude. The destructive narcissist appears to feel that they have a right to exploit others. Exploitation may also be associated with their understanding that others are simply extensions of them, where the exploiter does not have a good sense of where they end and others begin. Therefore, others are under their control and only exist to be of service to them. They simply feel that it's okay to lie, cheat, mislead, or manipulate since they must be served, enhanced, and preserved, and others should be happy to do whatever is needed.

This person may also become very angry when others don't meet their expectations. They are likely to drop friends, ignore colleagues, and/or try to destroy others who refuse to be exploited, and there are some who'll do the same to their child who refuses to be exploited. But what's more likely is that they will resort to emotional blackmail, try to indirectly manipulate the child via another person, and/or promote shame and guilt.

They may also be shameless and ruthless in the pursuit of their aims. They don't seem to care at all about others' needs and desires—only theirs matter. They are often skilled at rationalizing whatever they do and escaping any shame or guilt. Don't be fooled by any expressions of shame or guilt, as they do not really mean it. This person will do or say whatever they feel they can get away with to attain what they want.

Emotionally Abusive

There are numerous ways to be emotionally abusive. The destructive narcissistic parent is very adept at knowing sore spots, emotional triggers, and exactly how to induce shame and guilt. Some are emotionally abusive under the guise of being helpful. For example, the parent who takes the carving knife from you, saying that they will cut the roast as you are so clumsy you'll wind up cutting yourself and ruining dinner. That does not change the negative impact of the emotional abuse, which seems to continue even into adulthood.

It's simply not possible to list all the ways that a parent can be emotionally abusive, but following are some behaviors indicative of emotional abuse. Rate the extent to which your parent does the following.

1. Makes demeaning comments about your appearance or abilities

2. Blames you for their discomfort or for not meeting their expectations

3. Criticizes you

4. Devalues you and your accomplishments

5. Belittles your efforts to please them

6. Makes unflattering and unfair comparisons with others

7. Disparages you

8. Suggests that whatever you do or say is never quite right

9. Attacks without provocation

10. Keeps you on the defensive

People who are emotionally abusive have several goals. Two major goals are the control of others and the support of their self-concept. Because you function as an extension of them, the more they can be satisfied with you, the more they are satisfied with "self." Basically, they are dissatisfied with their self, have an impoverished self-concept, and are trying to attain perfection. As an extension of this self, you are satisfying when you meet this self-perception of perfection (what they want you to be, do, or say) and dissatisfying when you do not meet the expectation.

The destructive narcissistic parent appears to be totally insensitive or oblivious to the impact of their words on you. Everyone else can see the visible discomfort or pain you display during the abuse, but that does not seem to make any difference to them. They continue to say hurtful and rejecting things. And remember, they may also have a lack of empathy which means they're not likely to have an appreciation of the impact of their words on you. It's interesting and frustrating to note that these are the same people who could never tolerate anyone saying these things to them.

You, as a child and as an adult, are in a subordinate position to the parent. They can say abusive things to you, and you are expected to take it. The parent will not tolerate any protests, generally deeming them as "sass," talking back, being disrespectful, or being "oversensitive." You basically have to stand there and receive whatever they dish out. Years of this behavior can be terribly eroding to your self-confidence and self-esteem.

Your Parent's Rating

What did you find out? Did your parent(s) have numerous behaviors and attitudes indicative of destructive narcissism? Did you find yourself reliving some times that were frustrating, humiliating, or wounding? Are you angry as you read this? It would not be unusual for you to have old feelings aroused and to be upset and angry when you reflect on the impact of your parent's behaviors and attitudes on your current life. You may even be asking yourself why your parent(s) couldn't be different, better, or perfect. If you rated your parent(s) with mostly 4's and 5's your parent most likely has a destructive narcissistic pattern. Look for high scores on four or more of the nine scales in making this determination.

Gaining Perspective

So, let's take a few moments to put what you are experiencing into perspective. Before reading any further, let's try to deal with some of the unpleasant emotions that may have come up.

1. Sit in silence in a comfortable position.

2. Close your eyes.

3. Concentrate on your breathing and try to consciously make it deep and even.

4. Do this for two to three minutes.

5. Do not try to change your thoughts—just let them flow through your mind.

6. If you find that something persists and increases your anger, concentrate on your breathing.

It's important that you do not try to minimize the impact of your emotions. They are significant, but you don't have to become mired in them, overwhelmed, or let their intensity increase.

Now reflect for a few moments on the positive ways you developed in spite of your parent's influences. You probably have many positive qualities, and these, too, were impacted by parental influences, as well as any predispositions you had. This is also important to acknowledge.

There is no doubt that parental destructive narcissism has lasting negative effects on the child. However, there is also no doubt that you, as an adult, can begin to understand these effects and take steps to counteract them. As you work through these effects and your feelings, do not forget that your destructive narcissistic parent:

- is unaware of their destructive narcissistic behaviors and attitudes

- generally assumes that everyone else is like them

- sees no need to change

- will not respond to confrontation

- did the best they could as a parent.

These are all very simple points, but you may find it difficult to accept and remember them. You may have some unrealistic expectations that your parent will change if they could only:

- understand what they are doing

- accept what you and others say about their behaviors and attitudes

- accept responsibility for their behaviors and attitudes

- understand your feelings

- consider you a separate individual

- want to change.

If you can begin to accept and remember the points in the first list, you will find that you are less frustrated, angry, and confused, and you will be able to increase your ability to effectively cope with your destructive narcissistic parent.

The remainder of the book presents strategies to help cope with destructive narcissistic parents. The strategies focus on you, not your parents. You will have to sort through the suggestions and use those that best fit your personality and circumstances. You may even be inspired to create some unique strategies of your own. The following assumptions guide the suggestions:

- You have the desire and power to change.

- You want to maintain a relationship with your parent.

- You want to react to your parent in a more satisfying way.

- You are interested in promoting growth in any areas of lingering underdeveloped narcissism you may have.

Chapter 3 starts the journey of self-exploration by focusing on persistent effects of destructive narcissism on adults who were expected to parent their parents or whose parents were destructive narcissists. Either way, the child did not get the parenting they needed and are still paying the costs as adults. Understanding what the effects are and beginning the process of change is emphasized, as is the futility of blaming your parents and maintaining the fantasy that the parent will change.

Chapter 4 begins the process of helping you find and use techniques to insulate and protect yourself from being wounded by your parent(s). These can be used as you work to develop your "self," so that you attain healthy adult narcissism.

Chapter 3

Adult Children of Parents with a DNP

Many experiences, combined with genetic predisposition, shaped you to become the adult you are today. Among the more important and significant shaping experiences are those provided by your parents. There are other significant and important influences, but the parent-child relationship is one of the most important.

Your parents influenced your psychological development from birth. Many or all of these early influences cannot be recalled by you because the "infant you" couldn't store them in memory in a form that can be understood as an adult. For example, you can recall actions, events, and feelings from childhood because they are stored in your memory in images and impressions for which you have associations and words. The same is not true for actions, events, and feelings experienced as an infant. Your inability to recall these can limit some of your understanding but does not diminish their importance.

If you grew up experiencing parental destructive narcissism, there are effects on you that persist and have an impact on your adult feelings, behaviors, and attitudes. This chapter focuses on an examination of these lasting effects as one avenue for identifying parental destructive narcissism. Besides helping you deal more effectively with your parent, another outcome may be that you gain an increased awareness of personal unproductive behaviors and attitudes that may be undermining your self-confidence, self-esteem, and relationships. You can't make your parents change, but you can effect personal changes.

The Impact of Your Parent(s) on Your Functioning

Following are some pervasive themes that children of self-absorbed parents can experience even as adults. This is the first of several ways to consider the lasting impact of some of your parent's behaviors and attitudes on you. The themes and the list following of how others may perceive you turns the focus from your parent to you. These lists will be revisited in chapter 7 but for now they are used to help you begin the process of self-reflection.

When you think of your life and self as you are at the present time, which of the following would be a theme?

- Lack of meaning or purpose in life
- Lack of a satisfying intimate relationship
- Problems in relationships with family or friends
- Problems with relationships at work
- Lack of self-confidence
- Feeling incompetent or flawed
- Lack of understanding and acceptance from others
- Feeling isolated and/or alienated
- Feeling overwhelmed by others' demands or expectations
- Feeling emotionally out of sync with others

- Insecure about your abilities to cope or be effective

- Often feel hurt and angry at unfair blame or criticism

- Generalized dissatisfaction with self.

If you identified several of the above as current themes in your life, you may be suffering some persistent effects of parental destructive narcissism. But, before we jump to that conclusion, let's take a look at how others may be perceiving you. Their perceptions can also provide clues.

Are you criticized frequently by others as:

- overreacting

- being detached or withdrawn

- self-centered or selfish

- insensitive

- uncaring

- expecting or demanding too much from others

- insecure or unconfident

- arrogant or cocky

- overbearing

- shallow

- touchy or oversensitive to comments by others

- considering yourself superior or inferior to others

- being overly responsible

- seeking the limelight or approval.

Others are not always accurate in their perceptions, but if you're receiving these criticisms from more than one person, and they occur over time, then you need to consider that you are indeed acting in a way that supports their perceptions.

Taking a Personal Inventory

Form 3-1 helps you look at some behaviors, attitudes, and feelings that characterize a "siege response" to having a parent or parents with a DNP. I call it a siege response because there is considerable energy spent in hiding and defending oneself from both internal and external dangers. Form 3-2 includes characteristics for a "compliant response." This response is the one used to ingratiate, cooperate, and meet the parent's expectation. Each item can be rated from 5, "I always or almost always do or feel this," to 1, "I never or almost never do or feel this." Reflect on your current behaviors, attitudes, and feelings and rate yourself on both scales.

Form 3-1: The "Siege Response" Scale

DIRECTIONS: Reflect on your usual reactions and rate your-self using the following scale:

5 - always or almost always   2 - infrequently

4 - frequently   1 - never

3 - sometimes

1. Become defiant when given orders, demands, or are told what to do   5 4 3 2 1

2. Rebel against rules and restrictions   5 4 3 2 1

3. Are wary or fearful of intimacy   5 4 3 2 1

4. Are unsure of what will please others   5 4 3 2 1

5. Feel emotionally out of sync with others   5 4 3 2 1

6. Are impatient or withdrawn from others' intense emotions   5 4 3 2 1

7. Feel anxious or panicky when others want or appear to want you to nurture them   5 4 3 2 1

8. Are fearful of getting overwhelmed or enmeshed by others' emotions   5 4 3 2 1

9. Are easily frustrated by authority figures   5 4 3 2 1

10. Feel guilty   5 4 3 2 1

11. Suppress feelings   5 4 3 2 1

12. Feel envious of others possessions, achievements, relationships   5 4 3 2 1

13. Are easily offended   5 4 3 2 1

14. Personalize behaviors of others   5 4 3 2 1

Form 3-2: The "Compliant Response" Scale

DIRECTIONS: Reflect on your usual response and rate yourself on each item using the following scale:

5 - always or almost always   2 - infrequently

4 - frequently   1 - never

3 - sometimes

1. Monitor your behavior to be sure it is acceptable to others	5 4 3 2 1
2. Need to be liked and approved of by others	5 4 3 2 1
3. Work hard to please others but feel unsure of what will please them	5 4 3 2 1
4. Feel responsible for others well-being	5 4 3 2 1
5. Sacrifice personal needs for others	5 4 3 2 1
6. Make self-depreciating comments	5 4 3 2 1
7. Want desperately to "get it right"	5 4 3 2 1
8. Have unrealistic expectations of self and of others	5 4 3 2 1
9. Are overly critical of self and of others	5 4 3 2 1
10. Are overly responsible	5 4 3 2 1
11. Have perfectionistic behavior and expectations	5 4 3 2 1
12. Are overemotional and over-responsive	5 4 3 2 1
13. Easily become intimate with others	5 4 3 2 1
14. Feel that others take advantage of you	5 4 3 2 1
15. Others are perceived as more worthy	5 4 3 2 1
16. Are easily offended	5 4 3 2 1
17. Work hard to soothe others' intense feelings	5 4 3 2 1
18. Personalize others' behaviors	5 4 3 2 1

The Siege Response

Scores on this scale can range from 14 to 70, with scores at the lower end indicating that these are behaviors, attitudes, and feelings that are never or almost never experienced and scores at the higher end indicating that they are almost always experienced. The higher your scores, the more you tend to react to protect yourself, not just with your parents, but with many others, including friends, family, and intimate partners.

This pattern of behaviors, attitudes, and feelings suggest that you are mobilizing your resources to avoid:

- being manipulated

- becoming engulfed or enmeshed by others' needs and demands

- feeling responsible for others' well-being

- feeling diminished when you do not meet others expectations.

The resources you mobilize to protect yourself are your defense mechanisms. You are defending against the potential threats of being manipulated, enmeshed, or engulfed by others feelings and of feeling flawed. Some of your behaviors are the outcomes of defenses such as:

- defiance

- rebellion

- withdrawal

- insensitivity.

Defiance

Defiance, as a defense, seems to occur as a response when others are perceived as trying to get you to do what they want you to do. It does not seem to matter what that the person is suggesting or telling you to do. Even if it's in your best interest, the inevitable feeling that you are being manipulated leads to mistrusting their motives and being defiant. There is an overreaction to the potential threat you feel of being manipulated to meet someone else's needs, of becoming enmeshed in others' feelings, and/or of feeling incompetent.

Defiance is an easily triggered response, especially when someone tells you:

- "Don't do that."

- "You can't do that."

- "Do that."

It is not always an overt response. There are times when defiance takes a milder form such as skepticism or a "wait and see" stance. Some sort of attack or manipulation is anticipated and must be guarded against.

Rebellion

Defiance and rebellion seem to go together. Whereas defiance is an attitude, rebellion is action. When you rebel, it is always against something, such as rules, regulations, orders, laws, or expectations.

Rebellion can take many forms, some of which are very destructive to you and/or others. All rebellion is not bad or wrong—sometimes it is the only way you are able to establish independence. Being able to successfully complete the process of psychological independence from your parents is very important in order to develop healthy narcissism, and sometimes rebellion is the only way this independence can be established.

Reacting in a rebellious way to rules and regulations can be destructive because this rebellion can have something of an indiscriminate character. This is especially true when rebellion becomes an ingrained response to almost everything, including some things that are in your best interest. The real message in this sort of rebellion is still being delivered to the parent ("You can't make me do that"), even if the parent is not ostensibly involved.

There is also covert rebellion, where you act against your parent's wishes or expectations in an indirect way. For example, the daughter who rebels against parental expectations that her life goal should be to get married, have a family, and not seek success by rejecting all suitors and establishing a high-powered career. Another example is the young man who, upon receiving his law degree, gives it to his mother, saying that this was what *she* wanted and that now he's going to be a policeman, as he always wanted.

Withdrawal

By far the defense most often used by those with a siege response is withdrawal. They react to threats of

- intimacy

- disapproval

- others' needs for nurturing

- others' emotional intensity

- the emergence of personal unpleasant intense emotions

- attacks on "self"

by withdrawing emotionally and physically. It seems as if they disappear, put up a wall, or in some way shut themselves away. This reaction can be very frustrating to others who may be trying to establish a relationship, making a reasonable request for what they want or need, expressing their feelings, or wanting to know what you are feeling. They are trying to make connections with someone who is fleeing.

What needs to be understood is that the person is using this defense because of the need to protect themselves from experiences that seem dangerously similar to those they had with a destructive narcissistic parent. They have not yet learned how to distinguish between a real threat and an old memory and are simply reacting in a learned way. For example, they will perceive all attempts at intimacy to be a threat of becoming enmeshed or engulfed. They fear being "taken over" by others, since their parent(s) did not allow them to be a separate person. The parent with destructive narcissism considered the child to be an extension of them and under the parent's control. The adult child's rational, objective self knows that the situations, people, and options are different from those of their childhood, but the fear is so pervasive and has been around so long that they cannot understand the differences on an unconscious, affective level. That's why they choose to withdraw.

When withdrawal is consistently used, that person can then be perceived by others as

- difficult to know or understand

- aloof

- cold

- constricted

- detached

which only serves to isolate and alienate them even more. Internally, this person may be yearning

- for the love and affection intimacy brings

- to gain approval and validation by others

- to connect and care for others

- to feel capable and strong

- to not fear emotional intensity

but their fear is so much stronger than their yearning that they cannot allow the yearning to be known.

Insensitivity

Items 4–8 on the form comprise this category. Individuals who tend to make a siege response can also run the risk of seeming to be insensitive. Their efforts to protect themselves can make them appear to be cold, aloof, uncaring, and indifferent. It may be that they do care, and do want to nurture, but they must first protect themselves against being sucked in by the other person's needs or emotional intensity. What may appear as insensitivity to others may be:

- a feeling of being out of sync

- anxiety or panic about potential enmeshment

- the lack of certainty about what others want or need

- a fear of becoming overwhelmed.

This is the person who, once their feelings become engaged, may have difficulty maintaining emotional boundaries. They experienced this with their parent(s) and they had a sense that they were taken over and were being manipulated. They did not know where their feelings ended and the parent's began, and this was very frightening. They may have even felt that they were at the risk of being incorporated by the parent, and thus would be destroyed. When the child is dependent on parents for their very existence and then put in the position of being subsumed by the parent but also having to take care of the parent's emotional and/or physical needs, it sets up a very scary situation for the child. It's not easy to overcome this long-term fear. What may appear to be indifference or insensitivity is generally disguised fear or even terror.

Feel Guilty

The tendency to have a siege response can also produce constant guilt feelings. The person is insensitive, withdrawn, rebellious, and defiant in an effort to protect him or herself but also recognizes that these defenses have a negative impact on others. It may seem a bit contradictory, but the person is sensitive enough to recognize the negative impact of their behavior on others but is convinced that the defense is necessary. They therefore continue to use the defenses, leading to guilty feelings for having to mount the defenses.

Suppress Feelings

Persons with a siege response may also tend to suppress feelings. They fear rejection, minimizing of their feelings, or even being told that they are wrong or irrational for feeling the way they do. After all, this is what happened when they tried to express their feelings to their destructive narcissistic parent. Past experiences, the fear of being judged, and an inability to trust the validity of their feelings all contribute to the habit of suppressing feelings. They feel that it's not safe to have or express feelings.

Envious

Smoldering internally from the effects of the self-absorbed parent, this person can be very envious of others' possessions, achievements, and relationships. The constant question they have is "Why not me?" They hide behind defiance, rebellion, insensitivity, and withdrawal and then wonder why others cannot reach them, or do not recognize their worth. They fight an ongoing battle between feelings of being unrecognized and worthless against a yearning for the unobtainable parental approval and love. They too want to be considered loveable and worthwhile but act in a manner that pushes others away.

Easily Offended

Having a parent who constantly belittles, blames, criticizes, and devalues you can lead to expecting others to do the same. The constant expectation that you will be found flawed and wanting can produce a sensitivity that considers what others say as a direct attack. This person is easily offended even when no offense is intended and others do not perceive what was said as attacking. Becoming offended is a strong defense against an attack. It is also a way to forestall any idea of attack. It is important to remember that becoming offended is a way to prevent any further hint of criticism.

Personalizes Behavior

The adult child of a self-absorbed parent can easily personalize what others say and do. They have become accustomed to picking up hints, intents, and expectations from the parent, as well as being expected to know what the parent wants or means without the parent having to verbalize it. This pattern carries over to the child's adult relationships and results in a tendency to personalize what others say and do. The child was able to survive by understanding that whatever was said and meant by the parent was directed at him or her, and that lesson is not easily forgotten.

Advantages of the Siege Response

There are some advantages for assuming a protective stance. Though many of the behaviors and attitudes can get in the way of developing and maintaining satisfying relationships, they do reduce the likelihood that you will be:

- manipulated by others for their benefit
- assuming responsibility for others feelings
- overly helpful and possibly being interfering
- taken advantage of by others
- affected by "emotional contagion"
- pushed into doing something you don't want to do.

This protective stance has provided you with resources that you probably don't want to lose, but it may need some modification in order to allow you to develop more satisfying relationships, feel better about yourself and your abilities, make more appropriate responses, and cope better with your parents and others.

The Compliant Response

Scores on this scale will range from 18 to 90. The higher the scores, the more there is the tendency to react in a compliant way. Compliant behaviors include:

- acting in a way that seeks to please others
- conforming
- harmonizing
- soothing
- feeling responsible for the feelings and welfare of others
- self-depreciating
- being deferential to others
- abasing
- self-sacrificing.

If you scored high on this scale you most likely spend a considerable amount of time taking care of others but also feel unappreciated and that your needs are not being met. However, you continue to put more effort in trying to please others in the hope that by doing so, they will eventually meet your needs.

Many of the behaviors, attitudes, and feelings exhibited in this response can be traced to your relationship with your parents from an early age. Most likely you were given the task of caring for the emotional well-being of your parent(s) but were never able to get it quite right, so you continue to try today. You will also find that pattern repeated in other relationships. Even though your efforts with your parent(s) and others are not resulting in satisfying and expected rewards, you continue your effort.

Monitored Behavior

Do you constantly monitor your behavior to make sure you are:

- pleasing others
- conforming to expectations
- being included
- taking care of others' needs?

If so, then it's likely that you grew up paying close attention to the verbal and nonverbal cues of a parent, looking for guidance to what will keep them pleased with you. It is common for children to get their cues from observing parents, but most will be somewhat indifferent to parental expectations at some point, focusing on their own needs and pleasures. This is why toddlers are defiant, have tantrums, become cranky, and so on. The parent who is in tune with their child and is caring for the child's needs will try to figure out what the child wants or needs. The parent with a DNP does not focus on the child and is more inclined to expect the child to meet the parent's personal needs. Since this parent is also likely to have some grandiosity (everything others do is seen in terms of self), the parent will then begin to assume that any "bad" or defiant behavior is a deliberate attempt to portray the parent as less than perfect. This suggestion of error cannot be tolerated by the parent, and the child is made to feel wrong, inadequate, ungrateful, and unloving for making the parent feel this way. Notice that the parent doesn't berate the child for his/her behavior, but makes the child feel "wrong" for causing the parent's negative feeling. The child, naturally not knowing any better, accepts this responsibility and grows up monitoring their behavior to insure that the parent feels adequate, perfect, and loved. This monitoring behavior becomes extended to others and forms an integral pattern for the person.

Need for Liking and Approval

Take a moment to reflect on the extent to which you go to gain liking and approval from others. Do you:

- say you agree with someone when you don't

- adopt another person's activities so that they will like you better

- act against a value or belief in the hope that the other person will approve

- join with someone in an action or event just to be part of the group

- put others' comfort ahead of your own on a frequent basis

- allow others to make decisions for you

- sacrifice for others

- engage in other actions designed to gain liking and approval?

If several of the above are descriptive of your usual behavior, then you may have a deep need that goes beyond the usual desire for liking and approval. A desire would indicate some limits on what you would do to get someone to like and/or approve, whereas a need would indicate few or no limits. Others' liking and approval are then essential for your self-esteem, self-confidence, and self-approval.

If you checked 4 or 5 on this item on the "Compliant Response Scale," you probably spend a great deal of time making sure that you are acting in accord with others' expectations. Any hint that someone does not approve of something you did or said will bring forth your increased efforts to please them, to the extent that you may also be constantly checking with them to ensure that you still have their liking and approval.

It is easy to associate this need with parental behaviors. For example, this need frequently arises in adults when, as a child, they were only liked or approved of by the parent(s) when they met parental expectations. The foundation of unconditional love, that their child is loved no matter what, is missing. Children of parents with a destructive narcissistic pattern do not grow up with an accepting parent attitude. Love, liking, and approval are always contingent on pleasing the parent and are not inherent in the parent-child relationship. Thus, some adult children of destructive narcissistic parents are constantly seeking what they didn't get from the parent, and are never satisfied with the amount of liking and approval they do get from others. This need seems to be bottomless.

Pleasing Others

Relationships appear to be much smoother and more satisfying when each person involved is pleased and each tries to please the other. This is one way that you can show caring. However, it's much more difficult to try and please someone when you're not sure what will be pleasing for them. If you marked 4 or 5 on this item, you may be in the position of expending considerable time and effort trying to please others, but are seldom sure if you're doing what they want or giving them what they need. You may also be constantly trying to anticipate what they will want or need, always feeling anxious about your ability to please them. You don't mind doing or giving whatever it takes to please, you're just not sure what that "something" is—and not knowing is the unsettling piece.

This attitude and behavior may have antecedents in the parent-child relationship, where the parent expected the child to "read their minds"—understanding what the parent wanted or needed without the parent having to ask for it. There may even have been instances where the child was berated by the parent for failing to meet their unspoken wants or needs and told that they should have known what the parent wanted or needed without having to be told. "I shouldn't have to tell you

. . ." may have been heard quite often by the child. The parent was only pleased with the child when they were able to read the parent's mind and give them what they wanted or needed.

The expectation of mind reading expands to other relationships when the child becomes an adult. The adult continues to constantly attempt to please while suffering terrible anxiety over whether they are doing it "right."

Feeling Responsible for Others

How descriptive are items 4 and 5 for you? Do you find that you are constantly doing things to take care of others and sacrificing your personal needs to do so? Have you noticed or been told that you're overresponsible? If any of these questions strike a chord with you, you may be reacting with others as you were expected to with your parent(s) when you were growing up.

Sometimes it can be difficult to gauge when it is appropriate to take care of others or to sacrifice your personal needs. All intimate relationships demand sacrifice of personal needs at some point. Taking care of children also demands sacrifice of personal needs, as do some careers (medical doctors, therapists, or any social service career). It can be hard to draw a line between what is actually needed and being overresponsible. However, if you are constantly choosing to take care of other adults' needs and, by doing so, push your needs aside, you're probably being overresponsible. You must judge for yourself if you meet this description.

How was this attitude and behavior developed? Well, most likely you grew up with the message that you were always to put others' needs ahead of your own, and this message has persisted into adulthood. It's now so much a part of you that you never hesitate to step in and take care of others, sometimes without their having to ask for your assistance. You constantly give to others. However, there may be times when you question why you are behaving as you do, why others feel they can call on you to sacrifice your personal needs. You may not feel satisfied with the outcomes of your sacrifices, and you may even wish that you could feel less responsible for others' well-being.

Self-Depreciating

Do you find it uncomfortable to accept compliments and admiring comments from others? Do you generally make a response to compliments that is self-depreciating or that dilutes the compliment? Do you frequently or constantly:

- minimize your abilities

- focus on your mistakes

- diminish your accomplishments

- want recognition for your achievements but are uncomfortable if you receive it

- downplay your achievements?

These are some ways that self-depreciation occurs, both internally and in interactions with others.

Some people grew up with the cultural norm to be modest and formed the habit of making self-depreciating comments to avoid being seen as bragging, having a "swelled head," or as feeling superior. If you are trying to be modest because of a cultural norm, you're internal state will be very different from that of someone who actually feels they don't deserve recognition or admiration. For example, the person who feels undeserving may, when receiving a compliment:

- want to run away

- shrink from contact

- feel the person is just trying to be nice and doesn't really mean what they say

- feel unworthy of the compliment

- be dissatisfied with their accomplishments because they were not perfect

- cringe.

These types of reactions point to an impoverished "self" that continues to be a part of the person's self-perception. The person feeling this way has deep and profound feelings of inadequacy, believing that they're very flawed. They will tend to focus more on deficiencies, flaws, weaknesses, and errors than on their more positive characteristics. While it's admirable to try and improve, it is self-defeating not to also be accepting and pleased about what you do or who you are.

Growing up with parental destructive narcissism can lead to these types of feelings and responses, in part because the parent(s) did not provide the child with the inner assurance that is the bedrock of self-confidence and self-acceptance. Mistakes by the child were punished in some way that indicated withdrawal of acceptance of the child and blaming the child, not just their behavior. The child was made to feel that they had an inherent flaw that could never be overcome. This early experience contributes to their continuing attitudes and feelings.

Needing to Get It Right

When something does not go as planned or expected, mistakes are made, needs unanticipated, or others' expectations not met, do you chastize yourself for not "getting it right"? Do you feel that others have an edge on some knowledge you do not have that allows them to be more correct than you? Are many of your efforts focused on "getting it right"? If you answered "yes," then you may be reacting to old parental messages that are unrealistic. You may have been given the idea that it is your responsibility to make sure that:

- nothing goes wrong

- others' needs are anticipated and met

- you never make mistakes, wrong decisions, or poor choices

- you take responsibility for others

- something is wrong with you if you cannot always "get it right."

As an adult, you may recognize the impossibility of meeting this expectation of perfection, but that does not stop you from feeling devastated when things don't go as planned. You may also expend considerable time and effort in this endeavor, due to feeling responsible for others well-being, or to blaming yourself for not being perfect, but those efforts never seem to pay off as you anticipate or want.

Unrealistic and Critical

Have you ever been told by those closest to you that your expectations are unrealistic, too demanding, or impossible to meet? Do you set high standards for yourself and for others and feel constantly disappointed when the standards are not met? Do you feel that, no matter how hard you try, there is always a need for improvement? Are you critical of yourself and others for being or performing less than perfectly? If you find this is descriptive of your behavior and attitude, then you may have unrealistic expectations of yourself and of others, and you may be overly critical. These behaviors can have serious, negative effects on your relationships.

You may be telling yourself that you have high standards, and you intend to live up to them. In theory, that is an admirable goal and endeavor. Having high standards, however, is somewhat different from expecting or demanding perfection. High standards for performance are achievable; perfection, on the other hand, is unlikely. Thus, you keep frustrating yourself and others by trying to reach the unobtainable goal of perfection. This is especially true when perfection is expected or wanted for everything.

Old parental messages are easy to associate with these expectations and behaviors. Most all parents set high standards for their kids. When there is a parental destructive narcissistic pattern, however, many expectations and standards are unrealistic and unobtainable. Further, the child is made to feel shamed and guilty for not being good enough, for failing to be perfect, and for disappointing the parent(s). This is a constant message that permeates the relationship, not necessarily in response to a particular deed or behavior. *Nothing* the child does quite meets parental expectations. When the child becomes an adult, he or she continues to have the same desire to please and will make considerable and persistent efforts to be perfect. Of course, they'll never be able to meet these old parental expectations that are now displaced onto relationships with others.

Overemotional

Are you described as overemotional or oversensitive? Do you become intensely and easily upset, especially if you feel you are being criticized? Do you find that you tend to overreact to what others say and do? Once you access these feelings, do you have trouble letting them go? These are some responses that can signal your experience with a destructively narcissistic parent.

Overemotional responses can result from experiences with parents where:

- the child was constantly criticized by the parent(s)

- the child was not allowed to openly express negative feelings

- expression of negative feelings was punished

- the child was supposed to read the parent's mind and make appropriate responses

- there was inconsistent parental behavior and responses.

The child who grew up under these conditions is left never knowing what to expect, what is expected of them, and with the expectation that whatever they do is likely to be wrong. Overemotionality in adulthood can result from the constant expectation that others are criticizing them for something over which they had no control, and this deeply hurts.

If you tend to:

- expect blame or criticism

- perceive many comments to be devaluing of you

- are easily hurt by any hint of being mistaken, wrong, or in error

- feel that others expect something of you and you failed them, which means that you are flawed

- read criticisms as underlying motives for comments directed at or to you,

- feel a sense of personal failure when you do not anticipate others' needs, then you may have deeply held perceptions that lead you to easily overreact.

Easy Intimacy

Does your yearning for acceptance and approval lead you to becoming easily intimate? Intimate in the sense that you disclose sensitive, personal information, feel connected, and expect the other person to do the same? Intimacy also means sharing secrets, experiences, personal space, and/or physical togetherness. There can be physical and/or emotional intimacy, both of which include a lowering of boundaries and defenses, and a kind of merging and enmeshment.

Those who become easily intimate often:

- mistake the extent of intimacy desired by the other person

- allow their values to be corrupted

- can be manipulated by others

- experience profound disappointment when relationships do not go as anticipated

- violate others' boundaries without being aware of it

- can be easily taken advantage of

- give others ammunition to use against them

- are seduced into doing things they would not otherwise do.

A great yearning for acceptance and approval, combined with an inadequate development of personal boundaries, can lead to a pattern of becoming easily and inappropriately intimate. People who fall prey to this pattern run the risk that they will be exploited either:

- physically

- sexually

- financially

- psychologically

- emotionally

- or all of the above.

Feeling Exploited

Many of the previous behaviors and attitudes are also accompanied by feelings that others take advantage of you or try to exploit you. Do you often have feelings that others rely on your sense of responsibility to do things they could or should do? When something needs to be done, do you jump in and take care of it, only to end up feeling unappreciated and exploited? Do you feel that your needs are always pushed to the rear because you have to take care of someone else's needs first? Do you sometimes resent the way that others seem to rely on you and take advantage? These feelings may signal some discomfort with your overly responsible attitudes and behaviors, your need to work hard to please others, and/or your sacrifice of personal needs in favor of others' needs. On some level, you are aware that the return for your actions is less than acceptable—you're not getting enough for what you give.

It may be that these feelings are also similar to those experienced when growing up with parental destructive narcissism. You gave your all to the parent(s), but it never seemed to be right, enough, or really appreciated. Repeated and more intense efforts did not get you anywhere, either. Any protests were quickly put down by the parent(s), who used accusations, criticisms, blame, and exploitation of your love to quell your complaints. This repression led to resentment that was then suppressed or repressed by you. This pattern of effort that brought little or no payoff but did make you feel exploited and resentful was set early and continues in your other adult relationships.

Others Are More Worthy

Do you feel that the reason others

- get their needs met

- are successful

- gain acceptance and approval

- receive rewards

- are pleasing and liked

- do not have to work as hard as you do to be liked and accepted

- are able to "get it right"

is because they're just more worthy and deserving? Do you feel that your inadequacies and faults make you less worthy than others? That they are somehow superior?

There are times when practically everyone can accept that someone else is more able or adept in some area and deserves to win or be rewarded. They are deserving of the win or reward because of superior effort, talent, or ability. However, the feeling I'm talking about here is very different. The feeling that others are more worthy in this discussion refers to a deep and abiding perception that one's flaws and imperfections make one so inferior that others, by definition, are *always* more worthy. It's not what others do or say—their worthiness is inherent, just as is your unworthiness.

If you have or relate to the feelings that others are more worthy, you probably received that message from your parent(s). You were not given the assurance that you were loved and approved of no matter what imperfections you had. After all, imperfections are subject to individual interpretations. What one person considers an imperfection could be seen as a delightful quirk or as an asset by another. The failure to reinforce the child's self-perception, together with attempts to make the child conform to the parent's perception of "their child," can make the child (and, later, the adult) feel that others are more worthy.

Easily Offended

If you are overemotional, oversensitive, or overresponsive, then you are also likely to be easily offended. Do you feel:

- that others often try to put you down

- you are often unfairly blamed

- your mistakes are emphasized whereas others' mistakes are minimized or overlooked

- others are often trying to take advantage of you

- others are praised where you are criticized

- your faults and flaws are very visible and constantly being pointed out

- you are often devalued?

These are some examples of internal thoughts, feelings, and attitudes that can lead to your being easily offended. You may be perceiving slights where none were intended, or overreacting to any hint that you are not perfect. On one level, usually the rational, logical level, you know and accept that you're not perfect. However, at a deeper level, you are continuing to yearn for the unconditional positive regard and love that all children want and need from their parents.

If you grew up with parental destructive narcissism, then you most likely did not receive unconditional love and positive regard. The parent(s) could only approve of you to the extent that you met their self-perception and needs, and you were not considered to be separate and distinct from them. You were considered an extension of the parental self, and only when that "self" (you) met expectations did it receive positive regard. The parental inability to consider the child as worthwhile, loveable, a separate person produced a self-perception in the child that they are fatally flawed and that everyone can see the flaws. They, as adults, are constantly in touch with this self-perception and want to mask or hide it from others. When comments are made, this person immediately considers them to be a personal condemnation. They are acutely aware of their flaws and feel that others are also aware of them. This produces feelings of deep shame and leads to being easily offended.

Soothing Others

Do you join with others when they have intense unpleasant feelings to the point where you are also feeling that emotion very intensely? Have you experienced feeling others' uncomfortable emotions until you are ready to block, soothe, or prevent others from having intense feelings? Do you auto-matically spring into action to try and make others feel better at the least sign of distress? If you see yourself reflected in these questions then you may be continuing to react as an adult the way you did, or were expected to, as a child. This pattern may be especially true for children who were expected to take care of the emotional needs of the parent.

The rush to soothe others fulfills several personal needs:

- the need to protect oneself from experiencing others distress

- a wish to take care of the other person

- an attempt to satisfy the demands and expectations of a parental message

- a personal expectation for oneself that others' feelings are your responsibility.

Any or all of these may apply. You may be responding to internalized parental messages and/or acting in a way that highlights some lingering aspects of personal underdeveloped narcissism. That is, you're not yet able to adequately separate what is you from what is not you. Thus, you take responsibil-ity for others' feelings instead of allowing them to take per-sonal responsibility. When you soothe them, you are soothing yourself.

Soothing others can be very positive when done for rea-sons other than those listed above. When others are in distress they can appreciate some gesture that lets them know that someone is aware of their distress, cares about them, and wants to provide comfort for them. This is true for adults as it is for children. However, the quality of soothing provided is different. When you are truly trying to comfort them, you probably won't become as intensely involved in the other per-son's distress. In fact, there is probably some detachment: you will feel distress that they are upset, but not feel what they are feeling. Another characteristic of the quality is that you will not try to block or truncate what they are feeling so that you don't have to experience it. A very important characteristic is that you will allow them to have responsibility for their feelings and their ability to cope. You will provide comfort but not feel that you have to make the distress go away.

Personalizing Others' Behaviors

Do you tend to perceive what others say or do as direct or indirect comments about your:

- abilities

- competencies

- character

- appearance

- attractiveness

- loveability

- sexuality, etc.?

Do you often feel these comments are negative, pointing out inadequacies and flaws? Are you constantly feeling hurt that others seem to find these flaws and point them out to you in their comments? If the answers to these questions tend to be "yes," then you are most likely personalizing what others say or do.

Personalizing means that there is a tendency to perceive comments by others as attacks, criticisms, blame, or demands, and to feel hurt, defensive, and/or rejected. The person who personalizes seeks out what they perceive to be the hidden "real" message, which is really a disguised negative message about them. They feel that if the person making the comment were really honest, or would say everything they wanted to say, they would reveal their real thoughts and these would be negative. Even positive comments are examined for disguised negative messages.

The tendency to personalize behavior of others points to impoverished self-esteem. After all, how could others fail to see the flaws and inadequacies, or blame you for not being better or perfect, when this is how you perceive yourself?

Did you often hear any of the following from your parent(s) as you were growing up?

- "I shouldn't have to tell you that."

- "You ought to know without being told."

- "How could you not know that?"

- "Why are you so insensitive?"

- "You should be able to look at _____ and know what to do (they need, is right.)"

- "You saw me looking at you, and you should have known I meant you."

- "Even if I don't mention your name, I expect you to know that I want you to do it."

If any of these seem familiar to you, this can support the idea that one or more of your parents expected you to read their minds and react as they intended. This parent was also deeply disappointed every time you failed to do so and wasn't shy about letting you know that you failed and that you are flawed. After all, if you had been what the parent expected, you would not have failed.

This is an example of possible parental messages that led to the current habit and attitude of personalizing the behaviors of others.

What Can Be Done?

Basic information was presented in chapters 1 through 3 to assist in determining:

- if your parent was self-absorbed

- the effects of the self-absorbed parent's behavior on you

- your responses.

You probably re-experienced some of your childhood feelings as you read and worked on the forms and exercises. Your memories were not pleasant, but you allowed them to emerge in an effort to better understand how these were continuing to impact your behavior and relationships.

Chapters 4 and 5 present some strategies you can use to help manage interactions with your parents as interim measures while you build, develop, and fortify your "self." These strategies are termed *protective* and *coping*. Protective in the sense that there are things you can do to prevent yourself from being hurt by what the parent says and does. Coping in the sense that you can learn to better manage your difficult feelings (guilt and shame). This does not mean that you will no longer feel these unpleasant feelings or be negatively impacted by your parent. It simply means that you can work to reduce these effects on you.

Chapter 4

Protective and Coping Strategies

In this chapter I'll be discussing two categories of strategies, protective and coping. Protective strategies are relatively passive and call for internal shifts in perceptions and attitudes. Coping strategies are more active ones that teach you new ways to respond and behave that will be more effective.

One of your first responses to the ideas of developing protective and coping strategies may be, "Why do I have to change? They're the ones who need to change." This may be true, but the parent is unlikely to change because they probably see no reason to change. Another reaction you may have could be to want to try and make your parent aware of the destructive nature of their behaviors and attitudes. No matter how gently and sensitively you approach this confrontation, *it will not work*. Whether you tell them off or try to phrase a confrontation in a mild sensitive way, you will inevitably be made to feel wrong. Either way, you end up frustrated, resentful, and angry, and your parent still hasn't changed. Because their tentative hold on their self-esteem makes it impossible for them to truly admit to their errors, they simply won't acknowledge that this could be the problem—so *you've* got to be the problem. This is why, though you may have tried many things through the years to change your parents, nothing has worked. Thus, learning some more effective ways to protect yourself and cope can lead to more personal satisfaction and, perhaps, a more satisfying relationship with the parent.

Why Use Protective Strategies?

Protective strategies are thoughts and attitudes that puts up a barrier between you and the threat or danger. There are two types: protection against an external threat and protection within from experiencing intensely unpleasant emotions. External threats can be projections and projective identifications from the destructive narcissistic parent. The strategies I'll describe are defenses you can use at any time, but you may want to consider using them only with this parent or other destructive narcissists and not allow them to become an automatic response to everyone.

First you'll need to understand the nature of these external threats. What do the terms projection and projective identification mean? These are psychological constructs that describe processes individuals use to protect the "self." These are unconscious acts, which means the individual employs them without conscious awareness of what they are doing. Everyone uses projection and many use projective identification.

Along with projection and projective identification, there are three other terms used in this discussion that need to be defined:

- splitting

- identification

- polarities.

Splitting

Splitting means breaking off an unacceptable part of the self and either repressing it or projecting it. Either way, you get rid of something you do not like or cannot tolerate. When you repress it, you push it into the unconscious so that you simply don't have to acknowledge it. As far as you're concerned, you don't even have it. For example, suppose you cannot accept that you hate someone. You feel you are a very accepting and tolerant person and you couldn't *hate* anyone. If you used splitting and repression you would split off the hatred you have and push it into your unconscious, allowing you to say with complete sincerity and conviction that you do not hate anyone.

Projection

Splitting is also used in projection. However, instead of splitting something off and repressing it, the individual splits it off and projects it onto someone else. Then the first person reacts to the projected-upon person as if *they* had the split-off piece when, in reality, they don't. The projector reacts to their projection, not to the other person as they really are.

You may have experienced projection with someone who was angry with you. If, for some reason, this person finds their anger unacceptable, they may have split it off, projected it on you, and then accused *you* of being angry—when you weren't at all angry. Or, after projecting their anger on you, they began to react to you as if you were angry, leaving you confused about what was going on.

Identification

Identification happens when you resonate with something on an unconscious level and consider it to be the same as something you are or have. You not only see commonalties between you and the other thing, you may even incorporate what you see into your "self," for example, adopting mannerisms of an admired person. Identification is how we learn our "roles," establish our values before consciously choosing them, and become acculturated. An example is seen in how girls and boys adopt their gender-role identities as a female or male. Their first step is incorporation of a role portrayed by the parents or parent figure.

Since identification is an unconscious process, you will not usually know when you're "identifying"—it will just happen. Neither will you be consciously aware of the reason for the particular identification. Increasing your awareness and knowledge of yourself can lead to a heightened awareness of when you are identifying. You can have a better idea of those things with which you tend to identify and make a part of you.

Polarities

Polarities are opposites, such as:

- good/bad

- satisfying/unsatisfying

- right/wrong

- pleasant/unpleasant

- happy/sad

As we grow and develop we can become increasingly aware that there is a middle ground. Everything and everyone does not fall into one pole or the other—some are in-between or can vary from time to time. For example, infants consider mother as satisfying when she meets their needs and dissatisfying when she does not. As infants grow and develop, they generally become increasingly able to integrate these two polarities and mother is perceived as both. When growth and development in this ability is thwarted or delayed, the polarities are not integrated, and the perception of mother is that she is all satisfying or all unsatisfying. The inability to integrate polarities carries over to other things, including parts of the self.

The parts of the self that are split off and either repressed or projected are usually the result of unintegrated polarities. Whatever about the self that is unintegrated and unacceptable ("bad") is subject to being split off. For example, if one's guilt feelings are considered to be bad or wrong, then they will be either repressed or projected. The self cannot tolerate the feelings, so it gets rid of them.

Projective Identification

All of the terms I've talked about so far are also at work in projective identification. The way it works is like this: An unacceptable part of the self (a polarity) is split off from one person and is projected on to someone else. Then the other person identifies with the split off piece and incorporates it into him/her self. It's as if one person has tossed out an "unacceptable" trait, and the other person catches it and begins to act according to that trait.

And there is an additional piece to projective identification that occurs when the person doing the projecting maintains a connection with the split off piece. Because of this connection, even though the other person has incorporated it into their self, the projector is still able to maintain some control over it. Then, the projector can use that control to manipulate the person, making them act on the projected trait. Sounds complicated, doesn't it? An example may help clarify what occurs.

Suppose you are angry, but cannot accept your anger. You split if off, project it on another person, and they identify with the anger. Up to this point, they are not actively angry, even though they've identified with your anger. But, since you have maintained some control of your projected anger, you are now able to manipulate the person so that they become angry. You've managed to get rid of your anger and to make the other person act it out for you. You can walk away without carrying any anger, while the other person is left angry and confused, wondering how on earth they became so angry. The whole time, neither of you is consciously aware of what took place.

Another example of projective identification is seen when you are in an argument with someone, and your annoyance or anger increases to the point where some part of you is asking, "What's going on? Why am I this angry? It doesn't warrant my feeling this intensely."

What could be happening is that the other person has projected his/her anger, you incorporated it, and you're now acting on it. The anger is both what you generated and what the other person projected onto you, intensifying the anger you already had. All this is unconscious on both your parts.

Protective Strategies—What They Are and Why You Need Them

A destructive narcissistic parent is likely to have powerful projections and to be able to use projective identifications very effectively because of the parent-child relationship. As a child you were more open to the parent, including being open to their projections and identifying with them. This openness will tend to continue into adulthood.

Hatfield, Cacioppo, and Rapson (1994) write in their book *Emotional Contagion* about studies that demonstrate that babies "catch" their parents' emotions. Some adults remain very emotionally susceptible to catching others' emotions. If you are still operating under the parent-child dynamic and remain emotionally susceptible, you are wide open to catching the emotions projected on you by a parent. You will also be more likely to identify with projected emotions and thus will be more susceptible to their projective identifications.

The result can be that you are constantly trying to deal with your parent's projections and projective identifications as well as your own feelings triggered by interactions with them. All this is taking place on an unconscious level, which makes it even more difficult for you to manage. It will be helpful if you can learn how to recognize others' projections, understand when your emotions are triggered, and learn ways to prevent being manipulated by your identification with others' emotions.

There are several effective ways to deal with projections, projective identifications, and your triggered emotions. The most effective way is to work with a competent, qualified therapist to gain a better understanding of your issues, work through unfinished business, and develop more self-awareness. This self-exploration can help you better sort out what feelings are yours and related to your issues and what feelings are projected on you by others. You can also become more aware of what you tend to identify with most often.

There are also other strategies you can employ on your own that can help protect you from parental projections and projective identifications. These are:

- developing emotional insulation

- identifying irrational and unproductive attitudes and thoughts you have about your self

- increasing your awareness of how to intervene to prevent your unpleasant emotions from escalating.

Emotional Insulation

Just as insulation in a house helps to prevent heat or cooling from escaping or from getting in, emotional insulation can help keep projective identifications from getting in. You are setting up a barrier so that others' emotions do not trigger or intensify your corresponding emotions. For example, anger is projected on you, you already have some anger and, if you don't take steps to prevent it, the projected anger will intensify your own anger. Emotional insulation can prevent this from happening. Another example could be when anger is projected on you but you're not angry at all. Emotional insulation could prevent the other person from using the projected anger to manipulate you into becoming angry.

Emotional insulation should be carefully developed, because if it becomes a habit and employed unconsciously, you will find that you're blocking some feelings you may want to experience. Unconscious emotional insulation can also reduce your ability to be empathic. You will find it more helpful to consciously employ emotional insulation when you need it— especially in interactions with a destructive narcissistic parent.

Another point to remember is that you should *always* keep the emotional insulation in place when interacting with the destructive narcissistic parent. They tend to employ projection and projective identification at any moment and without warning. If you do not keep the insulation in place, you will find that they can easily breach your defenses.

Developing Your Emotional Insulation

In some ways, what you develop as emotional insulation will be very personal and individualized. You have to determine what works for you. Following are some suggestions for developing and employing your emotional insulation.

The first step is to visualize a barrier you feel would provide a barrier to other's projections. The image that works for me is one of massive steel doors clanging shut. Nothing dangerous or threatening can get through those doors when they are closed. A colleague uses a shade that he can pull down between him and the person. There are many barriers that could work well, including:

- a brick wall

- electrified wire

- barbed wire

- mirrors that reflect back the projections

- a force field

- a jungle

- a shield

- a suit of armor

or whatever seems appropriate for you.

Once you have settled on your image, you will need to practice it so you can become adept at quickly employing it. To fix the image:

- sit in silence

- close your eyes

- allow the image to emerge

- carefully explore all details of the image

- visualize it opening and closing or coming and going.

Try to *feel* the strength of the material you've chosen. Is it smooth, hard, soft, rough, hot, or cold? How large is it? What is its shape? What color is it? This is your image—you can make it anything you wish.

It really helps to employ the image prior to any interaction with the destructive narcissistic parent. It's usually too late to try and use it after you become upset. So, before meeting your parent, quickly visualize your emotional insulation. Remind yourself that it is very strong and will protect you.

The destructive narcissistic parent is projecting unwanted and unacceptable parts of themselves on you. When the projections get through and you identify with them, you wind up feeling those unpleasant feelings that they could not accept or tolerate. They feel fine, because they no longer have these feelings, but you are left with intense feelings that do not easily dissipate. Emotional insulation can help prevent the feelings from getting through to you.

Monica's story may provide additional explanation.

Monica

Monica dreaded interactions with her father as she seemed to always end up arguing with him and staying churned up and upset long afterward. Her stomach always hurt after even the shortest interaction with her father.

Monica knew that she would have to interact with her father at the family's holiday dinner. After arriving at the house, she sat in her car and quickly concentrated on her breathing, trying to make it deep and even. She closed her eyes and visualized her emotional insulation, which was a shiny six-foot-tall steel shield. She visualized it for ten seconds.

When Monica left after dinner, her stomach did not hurt. She wasn't upset and had managed not to get angry with her father, although he said some of the same hurtful things he usually said. On this occasion, every time he spoke to her she "felt" the shield between them. No projective identifications got through to her this time.

Visualization for Triggered Feelings

The other protection that can be useful is protecting yourself from experiencing some unpleasant feelings that are likely to be triggered by interactions with the destructive narcissistic parent. These are feelings that can be anticipated but most often emerge unexpectedly.

For example, you may have pledged to yourself that you wouldn't get angry, regardless of what your parent did or said. However, no matter how hard you tried not to react, you weren't successful. You became furious and kept the feeling for a long time. You may find that even thinking about a past or upcoming interaction is enough to arouse anger, fear, dread, or other unpleasant feelings. It sure would be nice not to have the feelings or fear having them.

Chapter 5 discusses some major unpleasant feelings people commonly experience, along with some strategies and exercises for understanding and managing them. These are longer-term strategies that develop your self-understanding to the point where it becomes much more difficult for your parent or anyone else to trigger them in you.

The visualization exercise (4-1) on page 74 is a helpful, short-term strategy to work with until your development of self-understanding increases. It will help you make interactions with the destructive narcissistic parent more tolerable. Use the visualization with your emotional insulation to shield yourself against projections and projective identifications, giving yourself the time to assess what is happening, both internally and externally. This time gives you an opportunity to do one or more of the following:

- Tune in and identify the level of feeling you're experiencing

- Affirm to yourself that you don't have to let the feeling intensify or accelerate

- Remind yourself that you are an adult and not a child

- Become analytical and try to identify the projection, or block the feeling and tell yourself that you will deal with it later.

Exercise: A Place of Peace

This is a short imaging or visualization exercise. When you "image" something, or create it in your imagination, it is uniquely yours. You'll find it helpful if you can just let the images emerge and not try to edit or change them. Do not evaluate the images as good or bad—they all tell you something of value. The final point about imaging or visualization is that you can stop the imaging at any time by opening your eyes. Once you establish your "peaceful place," you can go there at any time and use its calming effects.

1. Sit in silence and allow your breathing to become deep and even.

2. Try to become aware of where the tension is in your body and release it.

3. Allow the words, "My peaceful place," to form images. Do not sort, change, or evaluate the images.

4. Note details of the spot, like colors, sounds, smells, temperature, and other sensations.

5. Focus on you and what you experience in your peaceful place.

6. When you're ready, come back to the room and open your eyes.

Nonverbal Emotional Insulation

There are some nonverbal behaviors that may be helpful in maintaining your emotional insulation. Some may be irritating to the receiver or observer and you should use them with full awareness that your intent is to irritate. When used this way, the resulting irritation is a form of retaliation. You are consciously deciding to exact revenge on the parent. Some parents will become so irritated that they leave you alone. Others will increase their attacks. The cost to you may be more than you wish to pay and that is why you must carefully consider what you are doing before acting.

If you're using any of the nonverbal insulating behaviors to protect yourself and that results in irritating the parent, you may have to accept that the parent would have become irritated no matter what you did, even if you were to be agreeable and cooperative. The primary goal for using any verbal or non-verbal insulating behavior is to protect yourself from the more distressing behaviors and attitudes of your self-absorbed parent.

The behaviors are:

- Keeping your distance

- Facial expressions and arm positions

- Hand movements

- Use of the body.

The further away you stand or sit from someone, the less intimacy can be develop or forced. The social zone is four-to-twelve feet and is used for strangers and people we don't know well. Try standing and sitting at least four feet from the destructive narcissistic parent. Make a habit of sitting across from them, not beside them.

Facial expressions can be very revealing of one's inner experience. Once you become aware of your facial expressions, you can school yourself to be less revealing of your inner thoughts and feelings. Practice assuming and holding a "sober face" or "poker face." That's one that is intended to not give clues to your thoughts and feelings—a blank expression. By concentrating on keeping your face blank, you are less open to projections and projective identifications.

Lack of eye contact, flat eye contact, and gazing at a spot between the eyes reduces intimacy. The more intimate you are with the destructive narcissistic parent, the more you put yourself in a position to identify with their projections, be manipulated into acting on them, and experience unpleasant emotions.

There are several hand and arm positions and movements that can convey disinterest, defiance, and confidence. Most all are irritating.

- Raised hand steeple: the tips of the fingers touch each other and the hands are at chest level or under chin (conveys confidence)

- Cross your arms and/or grip your upper arms (conveys defiance and resistance)

- Palms of hands down (conveys defiance)

- Picking lint (conveys disinterest and indifference).

Use the following body positions to convey dominance, indifference, or disinterest.

- Orient your body away from the destructive narcissistic parent when they are talking.

- Use little body movement. Movement conveys anxiety.

- Lean backwards with hands clasped behind the head.

These visualization and nonverbal emotional insulation strategies can be helpful in protecting you from both your internal triggered feelings and from the hurtful words and attitudes of your destructive narcissistic parent. You can use the next set of strategies to work on your attitudes and behaviors.

Coping Strategies

Protective strategies are coping strategies too, but I use the term specifically here to mean actions you can take and attitudes you can change that will let you to have more satisfying interactions and relationships with your destructive narcissistic parents. These are active steps you can take that will also further your personal growth and development. Coping strategies are also empowering, making you feel more grounded, competent, and in control of yourself—less like a victim.

Included with coping strategies is learning to avoid certain behaviors and attitudes. These specific behaviors and attitudes are counterproductive with a destructive narcissist and have the added effect of leaving you even more upset and confused. Chief among those to avoid are confrontation and trying to empathize. There are also some fantasies you may have that aren't helpful to you. You may not consider them "fantasies"—maybe they are dreams or wishes for how you'd like things to be with your parent. As much as it may hurt, it's really best to give up these hopes and dreams.

Change Attitudes

One strategy that can really help you cope is to change some unproductive and less-than-constructive attitudes you may have. The following scale is designed to assess the degree to which you have some attitudes that, if changed, would help you better cope with your destructive narcissistic parent.

Rate the extent to which you have, or act on, the following attitudes using the following scale: 5—I always or almost always think or feel this; 4—I frequently feel or think this; 3—I sometimes feel or think this; 2—I seldom feel or think this; and 1—I never or almost never think or feel this.

Ineffective Attitudes Scale

1. Everyone is always out to "get" me or take advantage of me.

2. I should be ashamed when I disappoint my parents or anyone else.

3. My needs are always secondary to others' needs.

4. Everything must be done my way.

5. I should not make mistakes.

6. It's awful when others feel distress and I must do something to prevent or stop them from feeling that way.

7. When someone criticizes me, they are trying to destroy me, and I must feel profoundly ashamed and/or fight back and try to destroy them.

8. I must always compare my behavior to others to make sure I am doing the right thing.

9. If I don't take steps to prevent it, I will become overwhelmed by others' intense feelings.

10. If I let someone get close or intimate, they will hurt me.

11. When someone rejects my ideas, they are rejecting me.

12. I need the approval of others in order to feel accepted.

13. If I don't get constant attention, I'm being rejected.

14. I can never "get it right" and should be profoundly ashamed.

15. I should love and honor my parents at all times and under all conditions.

16. I deserve to have _____ more than _____ does.

Scores can range from 16 to 80. The higher your score, the more often you exhibit these self-defeating attitudes.

You probably are not going to be successful at trying to change all self-defeating attitudes at once. Give yourself plenty of time to make these fundamental changes, gradually moving to where you'd like to be. You may also want to explore how your behavior is influenced by these attitudes. For example, if you have an attitude that you can never "get it right" and should be profoundly ashamed, you'll probably find that you don't forgive yourself when things go wrong—even when they weren't under your control. Work on understanding and accepting your limitations, boundaries, and attitude of "doing the best you can."

Avoid Confronting

Confrontation is an invitation to the other person to examine their behavior and its impact on you. Confrontation is not done:

- to tell someone off
- under intense emotions
- to make someone change
- to feel superior
- as retaliation.

It's unlikely that you are able to use the following confronting characteristics with your destructive narcissistic parent, but they represent the most productive way to confront someone.

- Listening and clarifying what the person meant

- The absence of intense emotions on your part

- Paying attention to the impact on the receiver

- A lack of desire to make or demand that the person change

- A motive to help the person—not to accomplish something for you.

When all is said and done about confronting, even if you do it correctly, it probably won't work with the destructive narcissistic parent. This is because they absolutely cannot hear your concerns, tune in to your feelings, or accept that there is any need for change on their part. What's more likely to occur is that they turn it back on you and trigger your feelings of: guilt, shame, confusion, frustration, and incompetence.

What is puzzling is that most people continue to try reaching their parent this way when years of experience has demonstrated that it just doesn't work. You keep hoping that one day the parent will realize what they're doing and its impact on you, which will promote change on their part. It has not happened, and it will not happen—but you continue to put yourself through distress by trying over and over again. You can overcome this vicious cycle by making a pledge to yourself to stop confronting and begin using a more effective strategy such as emotional insulation, withdrawal, avoidance, fogging, and so on. This will limit your frustration and help you begin taking care of yourself.

Avoid Trying to Empathize

This next suggestion is not only difficult, it just may be impossible for you to implement. You may not even want to consider not empathizing with your destructive narcissistic parent because you feel that everyone deserves empathy. Besides, empathy may be the one way you can connect with your parent. Though, in an ideal situation, everyone should be listened to and empathized with, a parent with a DNP changes the rules.

When you empathize with someone, you open yourself up to experiencing the person's inner world. Being open means that you cannot employ your emotional insulation and you leave yourself vulnerable to being overwhelmed or engulfed by the projections and projective identifications of the parent. You essentially have no defenses when you empathize and, unless you have considerable ego strength, you run the risk of becoming so enmeshed that you lose sense of your boundaries. What can happen is that you become burdened with all of the parent's unpleasant emotion, much to that parent's relief. You end up carrying all of that intense emotion, unaware that you've even picked it up.

You will find it more productive and comfortable to sympathize or be understanding, but not *empathize*. For example, when your parent complains about something, you could content yourself with noting that the parent must be frustrated, or whatever the feeling is you think they could be feeling. But, instead of feeling it yourself, you remain detached, only acknowledging that the other person seems to have this feeling. You are sympathizing, but not jumping into the experience of their emotion by empathizing.

Avoid Self-Blame

It will be extremely difficult to avoid self-blame when dealing with a destructive narcissistic parent. However, it is possible to accept your mistakes without blaming yourself.

Blame is very shame producing and feeling shamed is very wounding. Your very "self" is attacked as inadequate, unworthy, incompetent, and flawed and this shaming also carries the implication that you can never overcome these deficits. Putting yourself in this position produces despair. Try to remember that you've only made a mistake—it doesn't have to lead to despair.

You do not need to blame yourself for:

- not being perfect

- failing to anticipate your parent's needs or wants

- appropriately meeting your own needs

- being different or less satisfying than others

- disappointing your parent.

Don't worry, you certainly will be blamed for these by your destructive narcissistic parent. But you can give yourself a break by not rushing to participate in the blaming game. Blaming is discussed more extensively in chapter 6.

Give Up Unrealistic Fantasies

You may have one or more fantasies that are counterproductive and you will have to relinquish them if you are to grow and develop. You may feel that you are giving up hope but try to realize that these fantasies give only false hope—they can never become real.

What are some counterproductive fantasies you may have? All start with, "If only _____, then everything would be okay." Fill in the blank with any of the following statements that fit your fantasy:

- My destructive narcissistic parent will change.

- My parent will accept me as I am.

- My family can be "perfect."

- I did not make mistakes.

These are fantasies because they will never happen. Your destructive narcissistic parent will not change because *they see no need for change*. The exception is when the parent, for whatever reason, decides to change and works to change with a therapist. But your fantasy probably includes a miraculous transformation for the parent after understanding the impact of their behavior on you, caring about you, and wanting to change for you.

Wanting your parent to accept you as you are is very reasonable. However, with a parent who is a destructive narcissist, this is very unlikely to happen. The yearning may never go away, but it can lessen. What is helpful for you is to be able to accept yourself and become accepting of your parent as they are.

No one's family is perfect and wanting or expecting your family to be perfect is unrealistic and unproductive. Even the most loving and close family is not perfect. What makes them different is that members get their major needs met most of the time. Members are caring, accepting, tolerant of differences, and are allowed to be individuals. As you can see from this description, the family with a destructive narcissistic parent just won't have these characteristics. Your family cannot approach this ideal because:

- the destructive narcissist is more focused on getting his/ her needs met rather than focused on their child's needs

- they consider the child an extension of self and not a separate, distinct individual

- they expect the child to anticipate and meet the parent's needs.

Working to reduce making mistakes is realistic. Expecting that you will *never* make mistakes is unrealistic. One of the most distressing things about a destructive narcissistic parent is their expectation that, as an extension of the parent, the child will not make mistakes. Once you realize that this unrealistic expectation is a fantasy you can become more self-accepting.

Expecting the Parent to Change

The hope that your destructive narcissistic parent will change will have to be forfeited. I can't emphasize this point enough—you cannot expect your parent to change. Though it may be painful to accept this fact, in the long run you will save yourself pain. Fix the idea in your mind and remind yourself of it as often as needed.

Meeting Your Emotional Needs

You will have to find some other way to get your emotional needs met, because your parent will not do it, either because they are unwilling or they are unable to do so.

As I noted before, the destructive narcissistic parent does not empathize. What generally happens when you attempt to get them to understand your emotional needs, with the hope that understanding will make them want to meet those needs, is that the focus gets shifted to *their* emotional needs and you, the child, end up trying to meet them. This dynamic leaves you feeling guilty for focusing on your needs but still frustrated or even angry that your needs remain unmet. Not only are your needs ignored, but you are also carrying some of the emotional needs for your destructive narcissistic parent. They feel fine, while you feel a lot worse.

It may sound harsh or cold, but you will be better able to cope if you can avoid looking for your parent to come through and meet your emotional needs. This also means that you will have to be more aware of your yearning for your emotional needs to be met so that you are not expecting others to function as the wished-for parent who would meet your needs. This is also counterproductive. You will have to learn new ways for getting your emotional needs met, like developing better personal relationships with others and parenting yourself.

Developing emotional insulation, changing attitudes, and avoiding behaviors and attitudes that are unrealistic and counterproductive are important protective and coping strategies. Some can be implemented with just a little practice, while others can take a considerable amount of time to fully develop. Select those that best fit your situation and personality. Keep in mind that you are using these for self-protection and not as revenge to hurt your parent. Try not to have a goal of making them hurt as they have hurt you. Make your goal positive and constructive and you will find that you:

- are less wounded by their comments

- do not feel guilty about not fully meeting their needs or expectations

- can be more self-accepting

- do not demand that they become different

- become more satisfied with yourself and with others

- increase your understanding and tolerance for them

- are able to have meaningful and satisfying long-term relationships with others.

In this chapter I suggested some strategies and techniques you could employ to better protect yourself from the distressing effects of you parent with a DNP and to better cope with their attitudes and behaviors. However, the most constructive approaches are to better understand that the parent cannot see what he/she is doing that is distressing to others, nor can he/she see any necessity for changing. You, on the other hand, do see a need for changing but must accept that *you* are the one who will have to change. You will have to change your attitudes, behaviors, and give up your fantasies.

The next chapter provides some suggestions for changes. You can change your responses to the parent and, as a result, change your feelings about yourself.

Chapter 5

Empowering Strategies

You may often have asked yourself why your parent does or says the things they do? Can't they understand what they are doing to you? There are no satisfactory answers to these and other similar questions. Telling you that:

- they cannot help it

- they do not see a need for change

- this is the way they are

- they cannot see what they are doing to others

- they do not understand.

may be of little comfort. Even if you were to accept these explanations, there is still a part of you that cries "Why?" You may never get to the point where you can casually shrug off the wounding comments from your parent.

However, you can formulate some attitudes and behaviors that will make the wounding less severe and deepen your understanding of yourself and of the parent.

Bipolar States

The destructive narcissist faces the world with two states that are bipolar: the grandiose state and the impoverished or needy state. The degree of personal development the parent has will determine the extent to which these states remain separated and at opposite poles. What is important to remember is that both states exist at the same time in the same person. So, when you experience the grandiose state in your parent, the impoverished state still lurks behind the grandiose mask. The reverse is also true; the grandiose state is present when the impoverished state presents itself as dominant. Sometimes the states are reversed during an interaction. This is one reason why interactions with your parent can be so frustrating—you're busy responding to one state, only to have them come back with the other state. They are totally unaware that this is what they are doing, and you are so churned up by that time that you cannot objectively perceive what is happening.

Only when a destructive narcissist feels

- omnipotent

- important

- loved

- powerful

- in control

- superior

is he/she satisfied. However, this person always has underlying feelings of

- worthlessness

- inferiority

- being threatened

- danger and being unsafe

- fear

- anxiety.

You have to respond to both if you want to be effective. Both states appear without rhyme or reason and shift on a seemingly capricious basis. This is one of the major reasons the destructive narcissist is frustrating and confusing to deal with in interactions. You respond to one thing only to find that they wanted you to respond to something else or to respond in a different way. Most often they don't provide clues as to what is most important for them, and/or it changes in a nanosecond. You may never adequately tune in to what they want, but you will be less confused and frustrated if you keep in mind that there are two states and you can't always respond to the correct major state for that particular moment.

Criticism and Blame

Very often when your destructive narcissistic parent criticizes or blames you for:

- not being perfect
- making a mistake
- not meeting their expectations or needs
- not supporting their inflated, grandiose self
- not accepting that you are an extension of them
- having a different opinion or perspective

you will likely have one or more of the following reactions.

- You feel unfairly accused.
- The parent has some facts or interpretations that are wrong.
- The blame or criticism is really the parent's but was transferred on to you.
- The parent is off target, and you don't even really know what is being talked about.
- "Where did this come from? It is so unexpected. This really hurts."

- "How could I be so stupid and insensitive?"

Quite often you are caught off guard and are at a loss as to how to respond. You feel churned up, upset, or angry, or may experience some other unpleasant emotion.

Even though you are an adult, your parent seems to be able to trigger your childhood responses to criticism and blame with very little effort. No matter how much self-talk you do, such as pledging that you will never let them make you respond that way again, you are unsuccessful. You may even try practicing new responses but when faced with your parent's behavior, you're unable to use it. You cannot break out of that box, and so you remain vulnerable to their charges.

You do have some alternatives, even though you may reject them for one reason or the other. You could:

- avoid all, or most, interactions with the parent

- employ emotional insulation

- become indifferent to them

- agree with the charge.

Avoid Interactions

If you are not in your parent's presence you can either escape being blamed or criticized to your face or reduce the effects. You can reduce the wear and tear on your emotions considerably when there is distance between you.

However, there are some negative aspects to avoidance that may outweigh the positive ones for you. Avoiding the destructively narcissistic parent may mean that you are also cutting yourself off from other family members (for instance, the other parent). You may also feel that it is your responsibility to maintain some sort of relationship with the destructive narcissistic parent and, by avoiding them, you feel you are shirking your responsibility. Still others may feel that avoidance allows the destructive narcissist to win, and they simply cannot be put in the position where they would "lose."

What may be a palatable compromise is to avoid many or some interactions. You can choose the times and places for interactions and even choose not to have one-on-one interactions. Having other people around can moderate some of the impact. Further, being in public may rein in some of their tendencies to criticize and blame you.

Emotional Insulation

Emotional insulation will work, but only if you have it in place prior to the interaction *and* keep it in place the entire time you are with the parent. This will shield you from the projections that can accompany blame and criticism and shield you from experiencing any intense unpleasant emotions that might be triggered by projections.

However, if you let your guard down, you will not have time to employ it again when faced unexpectedly with blame or criticism. The projection, triggered emotions, and/or projective identifications occur much faster than you can implement a conscious decision to use emotional insulation.

An additional constraint may be that you find yourself inadvertently shielding yourself from the other parent and other relatives with whom you want to connect. It may be possible to practice selective emotional insulation for different people at the same time, but I honestly don't know how that works or how effective it may be. You must weigh the benefits and consequences for using emotional insulation before choosing to use it.

Become Indifferent

If you have ever been on the receiving end of complete indifference, you can immediately understand how effective it can be. It wards off everything from the other person by conveying to them that they, their concerns, what they have to say, and even who they are does not matter one iota. It's almost as if they do not exist—the person is simply of no interest.

You could try being indifferent to the destructive narcissistic parent, but it will be difficult because of the long and intimate relationship between you. Real indifference could be built over time, but developing some smaller measure of indifference could help in the short term.

But first you need to increase your awareness of what indifference feels like, how you behave when you are indifferent, and your nonverbal stance or communication. You probably have never consciously considered any of these before, but then again, there was no need to focus on them.

Begin by getting in touch with someone or something about which you are indifferent. You neither like nor dislike it or the person, you are not attracted nor repelled, you feel very little. You do not care one way or the other—their existence is of no consequence to you. If they were to thrive, you wouldn't care. If they were to disappear, you would not care. There is no emotional investment one way or the other.

Once you have identified the target of your indifference and re-experienced some of the feelings associated with the target, you need to become aware of your bodily sensations, your facial expression, and your posture. Pay particular attention to your eyes. What you are likely to find as you examine yourself is that:

- your face is blank

- your posture is relaxed

- you are aware of no particular sensation

- your thoughts are elsewhere

- you hear words but not feelings

- you are aware of the person's or thing's existence, but that is all.

You really do not care if they stay or go, continue or stop, like something or not. You see the person, but you don't really perceive them.

Once you know what you do and feel when you are indifferent, you can begin to practice some of these in interactions with the parent. For example, you could assume a blank facial expression and let your thoughts go elsewhere. You could try to assume a flat expression in your eyes and tune out the feelings the parent may be expressing. All this is pretty difficult to do with a narcissistic parent, because they seem to be alert to the slightest hint of inattention and defiance. Once they feel you're not attending to them, this then becomes more ammunition for their criticism and blame.

Agree with the Charge

You also have the option to say you're guilty as charged, whether you really agree or not. You could say, "Yep, I did it," or "Yep, I am that way." If you agree with the charge just to get the destructive narcissistic parent to shut up, be aware that the ploy will not always work. Parents generally have the ability to discern when their children are jerking their chains. This can lead to more extensive blame and criticism.

However, if there is some modicum of truth to your agreeing with the charges, this may be enough to be satisfying to the parent. You don't have to agree with all the blame and criticism, just the part you feel to be true.

For example, suppose that your parent criticizes you for not calling or coming by often enough. Forget the reasons why you do not call or come by more often—they are important only to you. Your parent couldn't care less that you have new responsibilities at work, that you also have a family with small children, or that you are working two jobs. Bringing all this up would do nothing to moderate the criticism or make them more reasonable, and could escalate the intensity of the exchange. You can just agree that you do not call or come by often, defusing the situation.

Counterproductive Responses

There are some behaviors and attitudes that would be counterproductive and that you will find it best to try to avoid. They are unlikely to be effective because of the nature of destructive narcissism. Examples of counterproductive behaviors and attitudes include:

- trying to get the parent to assume responsibility that is rightfully theirs

- using logic and rational arguments

- letting them know that you are hurt

- attacking

- pointing out how unfair the charge is.

Think back to the description at the beginning of the chapter that presents the two states that coexist for the destructive narcissist—the grandiose and impoverished selves. The parent can operate from one or the other self, as well as from both at the same time. The destructive narcissistic parent is closed to:

- assuming personal responsibility

- any argument that suggests the parent was wrong or is making an error

- understanding your feelings

- your anger

- any charge of unfairness.

This person simply cannot tolerate any notion that they are not correct, are less than perfect, etc.

Also, when you look at the feelings for the impoverished state for the destructive narcissist, you can better understand why this person cannot accept personal responsibility, and so on. You will not like it any better, but you can understand that they need to rid themselves of bad feelings and project them on someone else, such as you. Since they cannot allow themselves to be aware of what they're doing, any attempts to illuminate the situation are doomed to failure.

What is most likely to happen is that the parent will find some way to turn it back on you. The destructive narcissistic parent does not fight fairly. He/she will bring up events or topics that are painful or sensitive for you, pull rank, or make you feel guilty for talking that way to a parent "who only has your best interest at heart." You cannot win under these circumstances.

Devaluing, Demeaning Comments

You may find it helpful to consider any demeaning and devaluing remarks by the destructive narcissistic parent as really being "self-comments." What the parent says about you is reflective of personal feelings about his/her:

- appearance

- values

- decisions

- abilities.

For example, if the parent were to tell you that you "look a mess," what they are really saying is that the parent is not satisfied with how *they* look. Their dissatisfaction is displaced on you. Even if you do "look a mess," the real message is always about them.

These comments can be very wounding because of the power the parent holds in the relationship and because, on some level, you may be fearful that the comments are true. They are tapping into your own self-perceptions and verbalizing them. Even if you do feel this way about yourself, you do not appreciate hearing it from someone else.

There are some responses you can make that will only serve to accelerate the emotional abuse. These are the responses you want to avoid:

- protesting

- showing that you are hurt

- attacking

- pointing out something unflattering about the parent.

If you were to protest, the parent would reply that they were only trying to help you and become hurt that you did not appreciate the effort. The parent may even be able to make you feel guilty about being "ungrateful" for the criticism.

If you show that you are hurt by the remarks, you won't receive any empathy or sympathy. What you are likely to encounter is an admonition not to be so touchy or sensitive. Or, the parent may ask why you can't stand to hear the truth. Either will be infuriating and even more wounding. Not only does the parent not understand what you are feeling, he/she says you are wrong for feeling that way.

An attacking response will initiate the emergence of parental authority. You will be charged with not respecting your parent, who will become very angry. Attacking may also bring the other parent in as support.

Pointing out a flaw of the parent is also ineffective as this will be seen as an attack or as a deflection. Further, since the parent does not accept the notion of personal flaws, he/she immediately rejects your comment as "sour grapes." If you use these tactics, you lose.

Some responses that can be effective are those that:

- flatter the parent

- defuse the intent

- turn the intent into a positive.

Before you can use any of these responses you will have to assume an attitude of not taking these comments personally and not allowing them to continue to deeply wound you. They will still be wounding, just not as much.

Flattery

Flattering the parent taps into his/her feelings of grandiosity and needs of being perfect and superior. Flattery is distracting and makes it less likely that the parent will continue their critical remarks. For example, if he/she comments negatively about your appearance, you could point out how the parent always look nice. If they comment about your values, you could respond that they seem to have clear values or are secure in their values. You don't have to agree with or accept their values—you are just noting that whatever their values are, the parent doesn't seem to have any questions or doubts about them. If the comment is about your decisions you could respond that you wish you could make good decisions like they do and you are working on it. Try to keep all elements of sarcasm out of your voice as you say this.

If the comment is about your abilities, you could respond in an admiring way about some ability the parent has.

Defusing

The intent of demeaning and devaluing comments is to displace personal feelings on someone else. The reasons for the intent are many and not really important in order to effectively respond. Defusing the wounding aspect of the comments can allow you to maintain your integrity, but you will have to have some measure of emotional detachment in order to employ defusing strategies.

Think of defusing techniques as taking the sting out of the comments. Mentally review previous devaluing and demeaning comments made by the parent and try to think of ways to defuse them. Of course, the best way to take the sting out of these comments is to not let them wound you, to let them slide off your back. But until you get to that point, you may want to try defusing.

One defusing strategy to use when your parent has begun cirticizing you could be to say to the parent, "It must be difficult for you to put up with _____ (whatever the parent found dissatisfying)." The parent will then begin to talk about their trials and tribulations, and you can think about something else. Another strategy is to ask them for suggestions in improving what they see as your faults. You certainly don't have to take the suggestions, but you do run the risk of having the parent expect you to follow through on these suggestions.

Make It Positive

Turning the devaluing or demeaning comment into a positive will take some effort on your part. In order to accomplish this, you will need some emotional detachment, a desire to use the positive part of any criticism and not be wounded by the negative part.

Making it positive means that you have to believe that there is a positive embedded in most criticisms. You may have to tease out the positive aspect, but there is probably one in there. Let's try a few examples.

Criticism	Strength
"You look a mess."	You have the courage to dress or look as you want. Not a slave to fashion or trends.
"You're such a klutz"	You're so involved in thinking, planning, organizing, and creating, that you become distracted.
"You'll never attract a man/women that way."	You will attract the person you need to, or will be content to be independent.
"You look terrible."	Your nonverbal behavior is consistent with how you are feeling. You are being genuine.

Once you begin to practice looking for the strengths in a criticism, you will find it easier to discern them and to be more accepting of yourself.

Manipulation

How does your destructive narcissistic parent manipulate you? Or, to put it another way, to what manipulation techniques are you most susceptible? What you may realize is that your susceptibility to manipulative techniques carries over into other relationships, giving others the power to manipulate you also.

Manipulation occurs when we are:

- seduced

- coerced

- blackmailed

- extorted

- tricked

into doing, believing, or acting in a way that meets the other person's needs. We may not even be aware of the manipulation when it takes place, only in retrospect. The residual feelings from being manipulated are:

- resentment

- betrayal

- self-doubt

- guilt

- shame

- anger.

People seldom, if ever, feel positive about being manipulated, even if it was in their "best interest." The manipulated person feels that they were made powerless in being controlled by the other person and couldn't exercise free choice. These feelings are eroding to self-confidence.

What are some examples of manipulation techniques used by parents with a DNP?

- Making the child feel that they will be loved, considered special, and so on, if they do what the parent wants

- Making the child feel guilty for not meeting the parent's needs or expectations

- Accusing the child of being uncaring or ungrateful if the child resists doing what the parent wants

- Withholding love, appreciation, and so on

- Making unfair comparisons with siblings or other children

- Coercing the child into doing something they do not want to do

- Telling the child that they are not reasonable and that the parent knows best

- Convincing the child that they would be bad and/or selfish if they do not do what the parent wants

- Threatening to broadcast something the child considers shameful.

What are some reasons for a parent to manipulate others? These are usually complex, involving several needs, perceptions, and attitudes, but they can be loosely categorized as:

- a feeling of entitlement

- the need for power and control

- fear

- believing the child is an extension of self.

Another way to categorize reasons for the destructive narcissist's manipulation is that it either reinforces the grandiose state or props up the impoverished state. The destructive narcissist is compelled to maintain the grandiose state and to keep the impoverished state fed, even if that means manipulating others. Others are not perceived as fully separate and distinct individuals who can be allowed free choice, respected as equals, valued for differences, and cared for as unique and special, and so they become ready candidates for manipulation.

What can you do to avoid or reduce being manipulated by your destructive narcissistic parent? Some of the most powerful are:

- rebelling

- becoming contrary

- setting guidelines

- disappearing

- highlighting the manipulation

- declaring independence.

Rebelling

You can always rebel and refuse to do something. This response is effective if done in a calm and reasoned manner. You'll find that it's counterproductive to have a tantrum or become irate when you rebel as that can make you look like a frustrated child trying to get their way. You will be more effective if you quietly rebel and simply refuse to do whatever it is, or say nothing and not do it. Noisy rebellion may backfire on you.

Becoming Contrary

Another behavior that is effective is to become contrary, doing the opposite of what is wanted or ordered or doing something entirely different. Again, you will be better off if you don't announce what your intentions are, but simply carry them out.

For example, say that your parent tries to manipulate you into wearing certain colors that they like. You could become contrary and wear all colors except those. A common example of parental manipulation is them trying to convince you to take on a specific career that meets their approval. Unless that career is what you want, you could choose something else, even if you have to scramble and find sources of funding for education and training. As any teen can tell you, there are countless ways to be contrary. However, you would not want to be contrary when it's not in your best interest. If your parent is mostly correct but is using manipulative techniques, you certainly wouldn't want to overreact to the manipulation by choosing something that is detrimental to you, just to be contrary.

Setting Guidelines

If the thing your parent is trying to manipulate you into isn't entirely disagreeable to you, you could establish some guidelines that your parent must follow in order to obtain your cooperation. For example, you could set a guideline of there being no hidden agendas in requests from your destructive narcissistic parent. The parent must become honest in requests to you. Consequences for their failure in being honest could be your decision not to do what is requested, or if only realized in retrospect, an unwillingness to do anything else requested. You could avoid the parent, refuse to discuss anything with him/her, or cut the parent out of your life for a period of time.

Setting guidelines is similar to confrontation, except that you are not inviting the person to examine their behavior, you are demanding that they change specific behaviors. You need to be aware that this strategy does not have much chance of success as the destructive narcissist does not accept that they need to change. Being direct and honest about your needs and demands will have little positive effect. You are more likely to be attacked or made to feel guilty.

If you can figure out a way to establish your guidelines and consequences in an indirect way, you have a better chance of being successful. This strategy calls for a high level of analysis by you, a willingness to engage in self-examination, and an ability to be somewhat objective. It can be very difficult to be this way with a parent.

To establish and enforce guidelines and consequences indirectly you must step back from the emotional content and:

1. Figure out how you are being manipulated.

2. Discern whether a request is honest or whether it has a hidden agenda.

3. Understand how the hidden agenda works on you.

4. Develop your personal set of consequences for their attempting to manipulate you.

5. Implement the guidelines and consequences.

In essence, you are turning the tables on your parent and are manipulating him/her. You must decide if you want to adopt that behavior, becoming more manipulative yourself.

Disappear

It's easier to avoid being manipulated if you're not in the picture. Just leave and do not return for some time. You can use this strategy at several different points. For example, when you realize that your parent is trying to manipulate you to do something you don't want to do, you could distract them and leave before you've agreed to their demand. Or, you could agree to do whatever it is, then leave and not do it. Finally, you can simply disappear before they get a chance to talk to you.

The parent will find it very difficult to manipulate you if you keep dematerializing on them. It will be like trying to catch fog. Just when they think they have you, you're no longer there. Disappearing works very well on the telephone. You could:

- hang up and say you were cut off

- say you have another call and hang up

- say someone's at the door and hang up

- say loudly "What's that noise?" and hang up

- say you have a bad connection and hang up.

These may be delaying tactics, but it gets you away from the current attempt to manipulate you. If this happens often enough, your parent may get the message that when certain topics are introduced, you disappear.

Highlighting the Manipulation

You could fortify yourself and point out to your parent that they are trying to manipulate you and invite them to be direct and honest instead of manipulative. In order to be effective, this would have to be done when you aren't in the grip of intense emotion. You would also have to be prepared for the backlash. Since the destructive narcissistic parent is probably not aware that he/she is being manipulative, or feels entitled to manipulate you and sees no need for making personal changes, he or she will likely be angry that you would even suggest that they are trying to manipulate you. He/she may say that he/she is hurt, to produce guilt in you, but he/she is really angry.

The backlash can lead to your feeling:

- self-doubt

- guilt

- anger

- frustration

- shame.

Once any of these feelings are triggered for you, you begin to lose control of the situation, leaving you open to other manipulation. This is why you must be fortified before using this strategy.

You may want to consider using this strategy as a step toward more complete separation and individuation. That is, setting a boundary and making your parent aware of the boundary and how you are no longer a part of them but are separate and distinct. Limiting the strategy's use and any expectations of immediate success will allow you to better accept your parent's response and feel fewer intense, uncomfortable feelings.

Declaring Independence

A declaration of independence will be effective only if you have an internal commitment to work hard to obtain independence and a willingness to accept the consequences. Simply declaring independence isn't enough, especially if you cave in because you cannot tolerate the consequences.

Independence is a process, and you must realize that it will take time to fully achieve your goals. You must be patient and not give up when you slip back into old patterns. Your parent will also be working against your obtaining independence.

How will you know when you are independent?

- When you can make decisions and not feel guilty about not consulting your parent.

- When you can either do what the parent wants or not do it and not feel ashamed for acquiescing or guilty for defying them.

- When you can objectively assess the parent's manipulation and decide for yourself if you want to comply for your reasons and not because of the manipulation.

Independence is obtained at a price. You may encounter

- emotional blackmail

- appeals to your sense of decency

- deliberate attempts to induce guilt

- demeaning comments

- accusations of ingratitude

- recapitulation of past offenses

and other unpleasant tactics. These are not easy to endure, but the payoff of independence can be worth the pain and effort.

It may be helpful to be working with a therapist as you go through declaring independence, as you can use someone to encourage and support you who can be objective and provide reality checks, and who can help you understand how your lingering aspects of underdeveloped narcissism are affecting your reactions and bid to be independent.

Protective and coping strategies are only short-term, stop-gap measures. Yes, they are helpful to keep you from experiencing the more distressing impact of your destructive narcissistic parent, but they are not sufficient to promote your well-being and to let you have a more satisfying relationship with your parent.

Chapter 6 begins the process of helping you learn ways to develop and fortify yourself. These are ways that you can:

- learn to emphasize and capitalize on your strengths and potentials

- reduce automatic reactions to distressing parental behaviors and attitudes

- promote personal development for lingering aspects of your personal underdeveloped narcissism.

Chapter 6

Build, Develop, and Fortify Your "Self"

There are many personal costs resulting from growing up with a self-absorbed parent and having to continue to interact with them when you become an adult. These costs may continue even if you only interact with them at a distance or infrequently. Their impact on your growth and development is significant, considerable, and long lasting.

The most powerful coping strategies are those that strengthen your self-concept, enhance your self-esteem, and promote your self-efficacy. In short, the most powerful strategies involve taking charge of your growth and development and working on those areas of self that did not thrive or were neglected because of the destructive narcissistic parent's inability to adequately nurture you. Their deficiencies produced your deficiencies—areas that need developing. Fortifying your self will enable you to better cope with your destructive narcissistic parent, maintaining a relationship with them even as you become your own person. Building, developing, and fortifying your self enables you to stop suffering from their wounding behaviors and attitudes and to address any lingering aspects of underdeveloped narcissism you may have.

Which of the following is most troubling for you in your relationship with your self-absorbed parent? All may be troubling, but you will find it more helpful to only address one area at a time. Select the one that is most important for you at this time, choosing between:

- valuing yourself

- accepting your limitations

- maintaining boundaries as a separate being

- the inability to accept and trust your parent(s) or others

- diminished emotional expression and access to your feelings

- the inability to forgive your parents

- yearning for your parents to be different.

Valuing Yourself

Growing up with a destructive narcissistic parent erodes your self-esteem, and this state can persist even after you become an adult. Their constant demeaning comments, refusal to accept you as a separate, unique individual, lack of sensitivity and empathy for you, and other destructive narcissistic behaviors and attitudes can combine to convince you that you can never:

- get it right

- live up to expectations

- be adequate and loveable

- overcome any deficits or flaws

- atone for mistakes.

Even as an adult you may still suffer these assaults on your self-esteem. It takes less effort on that parent's part to remind you of your flaws and inadequacies, as you are conditioned by a lifetime of experiences to react to certain cues—a particular look from the parent or a particular tone in their voice. You may not be fully aware of the cues or of your responses.

You did not get the valuing or reinforcement you needed from your parent early in your life that would enable your true self to emerge. You have to face the fact that the parent is very unlikely to change and that you must begin to give yourself any needed boosts to your self-esteem. A major task for you in your efforts to constructively cope with your self-absorbed parent is to provide this self-valuing. It will have to be internal instead of external—you will have to begin valuing yourself. A set of exercises later in the chapter focus on increasing your self-valuing.

Accepting Your Limitations

Some may find it easier to develop their abilities than to face their limitations. These are the perfectionists, the ones who obsess over "getting it right." These are the folks who are fearful of making mistakes to the point where they refuse to act because of this fear, and those who have an overdeveloped sense of responsibility. If this describes you, read on.

There is a difference between being able to intellectually accept that you have limitations, and the *actual* acceptance of limitations. You may know that your perfectionism, and hyperresponsibility are irrational on the "thinking" level, but on the "feeling" level, you're not convinced. So you keep trying to attain the unreachable, unrealistic, and irrational ideal.

Early on you probably incorporated a parental message that you were responsible for:

- others' feelings

- maintaining harmony

- doing better no matter how well you've done

- taking care of others

- meeting others' needs before meeting your own

- making your parent(s) proud

- whatever went wrong.

These messages continue to have an impact on your current behavior and self-perception.

Real acceptance of your limitations will take work. You will need to be vigilant about understanding your boundaries and about having others understand that you are separate and distinct from them.

Accepting limitations does not mean giving up, doing less than your best, or any other defeatist acts. You are not helpless or hopeless, you just have to understand what you can and cannot do and become comfortable with this. The exercises later in the chapter on personal limitations are suggestions for beginning to really accept yourself.

Maintaining Boundaries

O'Neil and Newbolt (1994) consider the following to be characteristics of people with healthy boundaries. These people:

- feel secure

- resist intrusion by others

- know their values, priorities, and perceptions

- appropriately self-disclose

- are self-confident

- can allow intimacy

- can be assertive

- do not become enmeshed or overwhelmed by others.

Knowing where you end and others begin allows you to choose your values and not have them imposed on you. You can better tolerate those who have different beliefs and values because you are not threatened by the differences.

Appropriate self-disclosure means that you carefully select the people with whom you reveal yourself, the timing and manner of self-disclosure, and are not pushed to disclose because of circumstances or pressure. You make conscious choices of what to talk about, with whom, how much, and you don't regret doing so.

Are you able to develop and maintain long-term, satisfying relationships? If not, one reason may be that you are unable to tolerate intimacy. You may be so fearful of having your boundaries breached that you cannot allow anyone through your boundaries to your true self. If you were made responsible for the parent's well-being, you are now probably wary of allowing anyone to get really close, for fear that they will do the same thing. You protect yourself from becoming enmeshed or overwhelmed. Your rigorous maintenance of strong, firm, unyielding boundaries can prevent intimate relationships.

On the other hand, maybe you have weak boundaries and can't develop satisfying relationships. Others may push you away because you do not clearly understand where you end and they begin. You become, or try to become, enmeshed with them, and they cannot tolerate this or do not want this. You may also suffer from exploitation because of your weak boundaries, both in intimate and more casual relationships.

There are times when you have to let others know where your boundaries are. You may have to speak up when people unwittingly or deliberately violate a boundary. How you let others know your boundary is important. When you can:

- ask for what you want
- say "no" when necessary
- tell someone they have irritated or offended you
- refuse to do something you do not want to do

you are being assertive. You have a clear sense of who you are and the limits of your responsibility to or for the other person.

Accepting and Trusting Others

Accepting others as they are, recognizing differences as well as similarities, respecting and appreciating diverse perspectives, and not being fearful of being overcome by others is not easy for someone who has experienced parental destructive narcissism. Trusting others is even more difficult, as trust develops from being able to rely on the other person, having confidence that they will not harm you and that they have your best interest at heart. The destructive narcissistic parent was unable to meet the child's needs and the child learned early not to rely on anyone other than him or herself to meet their needs. Even if the grown child is now seeking someone to meet their needs, they have a great deal of trouble bringing themselves to trust others because of these early experiences.

It may seem obvious, but I'd still like to emphasize that it is also difficult (if not impossible) for the grown child of a parent with a DNP to trust that parent. All hope may not be abandoned, but the child has received no evidence to date that the parent has their best interest at heart and wants to care for them. Indeed, all the evidence is to the contrary.

Accessing and Expressing Emotions

Do you have a wide range of emotions? Do you feel any emotion deeply other than rage or fear? Are you able to tune in to what you're feeling in the moment? Or do you feel stunted and shallow in the emotions you can access and express?

Our physical, psychological, relational, spiritual, and even intellectual sides are enhanced when we can access our emotions, have a wide range of emotions, and deeply experience them. The influence of our emotions on other aspects of our lives are often underestimated.

As a child you may not have been encouraged to express your feelings. You may have incorporated messages that the feelings were wrong, upsetting to the parent, an overreaction, or other negative messages. These messages have persisted and may continue to influence you as an adult. It may even be that you have suppressed or repressed your feelings for so long that you can't quite get in touch with, much less express them, anymore.

It will be necessary for you to learn more feeling words and increase your ability to express a wider range of emotions and to be more precise about what you are experiencing. For example, there are words to express gradations of feelings, e.g., irritation, annoyance, anger, rage, and fury. These gradations point out the different levels of intensity and give the receiver of the emotion a better understanding of just what you are feeling. All intense emotions have milder forms and having more words and phrases that are descriptive will allow you to better understand what you are feeling, express feelings clearly, and enable others to understand what you are experiencing.

The Inability to Forgive

The adult child of a destructive narcissistic parent will find it difficult to forgive them. The adult child may also find it difficult to forgive others who wound them. They hold tight to real or imagined injuries and cannot let go.

The hurt inflicted by a destructive narcissist is deep, pervasive, and lingering. Even when the now-grown child can better understand why the parent did what they did and maybe even be able to logically excuse the acts, the emotional part of the child still cannot forgive. The parent not only did not care adequately for the child, he/she did not consider the child's needs as more important than their personal needs. This causes a wound in the child that is hard to mend

It is the rare parent who does not make errors of judgment in child rearing. Most all parents look back and wish that they had done it differently and not made so many mistakes. This kind of reflection is common even among parents whose children have become fully functioning adults who are emotionally intact. These children can forgive their parents for mistakes. Children of destructively narcissist parents have a much harder time doing so.

As part of developing your self, you will have to come to some accommodation with forgiving the parent. It may be too much to expect to reach total forgiveness, but it may be possible to effect some forgiveness. Understanding that the parent was *unable* to act differently than he/she did may help with this.

Yearning for the Parent to Be Different

Along with forgiveness, you will have to give up the yearning for the parent to be different. That is an unrealistic expectation and very unlikely to happen. You will need to come to terms with your fantasy that some day the parent will love you and care for you as you need them to, and relinquish that fantasy.

It may sound extremely sad and futile to even read those words and think about the pain underlying them. You may feel considerable pain, but it can be worked through with the help of a competent therapist. That is the kind of work that therapists do best and, although it may take time and effort, the outcome will be worth it. That kind of work is beyond the scope of this book. What is important here is that you come to accept that you must give up unrealistic yearnings about your destructive narcissistic parent.

The exercises that follow are divided between this chapter and chapter 7, with the exercises to help you get grounded coming first and the awareness and choice-making exercises in chapter 7.

Each exercise is designed to guide the reader in developing personally relevant strategies to cope with destructive parental narcissism. But, before we dive into the work, I'll explain some of the nuts-and-bolts issues in doing these exercises.

Writing Exercises

The writing exercises are best done in a quiet place where you won't be interrupted or distracted. This includes telephone interruptions and distractions such as television. The choice of writing materials is up to you. I suggest using a loose-leaf notebook, a spiral notebook, or pads of paper, and pens or pencils. Some readers may prefer to use the computer.

Whatever medium you use, some provision should be made for privacy when writing and for the privacy of your product.

When writing, just let thoughts and images emerge unevaluated. You are not writing for anyone but yourself. You don't have to write complete sentences if you don't want to. Punctuation and other technical aspects of writing aren't really important, either. For once, you are free of any and all concerns about your final product. What's important here is *the process* of doing the exercises and what you learn from that process.

Pay attention to environmental concerns such as:

- room temperature

- comfort of seating

- lighting

- noise.

Once you become involved in what you're experiencing and writing, you may be able to screen out physical discomfort and noise. However, these environmental factors can prevent you from focusing at first, making it more difficult to become involved.

Some people like background music and others find it annoying and intrusive when they are trying to concentrate. If you like music, choose calming, quiet music. This is not the time for energizing music. Instrumental music may be more facilitating, as vocal music may have words that distract your attention. Whatever you choose, remember that music is also used in therapy to evoke moods and feelings. Your choice of music can have the same effect on you.

Nonverbal Expressive Exercises

Many of the nonverbal expressive exercises will involve drawing or creating collages. Even if you are unaccustomed to these activities, you may want to try the ones described in this book. Your artistic talent is not being judged and you should avoid slipping into self-judgment. Whatever you produce is okay, because the purpose for the activity is to give you an additional outlet for expressing feelings. Sometimes words are inadequate and limiting when you're trying to express feelings and these nonverbal exercises can really help.

Each activity has a specific list of materials. The drawing exercises will require paper and drawing utensils, like felt markers, crayons, colored pencils, or oil pastels. The size of the paper is important, so try to get some newsprint that is 12 by 16 or larger. Give yourself a lot of room to express your feelings.

The collage exercises require scissors, a selection of old catalogues and magazines, a glue stick or adhesive, and thick paper such as construction paper, poster board, or card stock. You may want to keep the drawing materials close in case you want to draw a particular symbol instead of finding it in a magazine.

Other nonverbal exercises are movement or body exercises. These are intended to increase your awareness of how your emotional life is reflected in your body and how changing your nonverbal positioning affects your mood and emotions. It is helpful to have a mirror in the room when you do these exercises, as the feedback you get from the mirror gets you more in touch with objective reality. You can then see some of what others see when they look at you. Of course, your perceptual perspective is subjective, but the mirror can help provide some objectivity.

Now you can begin your journey toward a more fortified self by starting with the grounding exercises below.

Getting Grounded

I use the term "grounded" here to describe the alignment of body and mind to reflect how a person perceives him or herself. It assumes, as did Wilhelm Reich (1972), that the internal, emotional state of a person is reflected in their body. The body's posture, movement, and positioning all mirror tension, resistance, and other internal states.

This notion of linking body and psychological functioning is extended here to help you develop better mechanisms for coping with destructive narcissistic parents. The exercises focus on your body posture and positioning, as well as using nonverbal communication to build confidence.

How can these exercises help? If you experienced any of the following as you were growing up and these acts persist even though you are an adult, then the exercise will help you build and fortify yourself to better deal with them. You can develop resources to help you cope when faced with any of the following:

- unfair accusations

- unflattering comparisons with others

- unexpected attacks

- the inability to predict what the parent will do or say.

Grounding Exercise 1: I Can, I Will

Objectives:

Set goal(s) for personal behavior when interacting with the destructive narcissistic parent. Fortify personal strengths.

Materials:

Whatever writing materials you decide you want to use; two three-by-five cards

Time Needed:

Varied

Procedure

1. Gather materials and sit in a quiet place where you will not be interrupted. The exercise is more meaningful if you complete it in one sitting. However, if that is not possible, considerable meaning can still be gained.

   Begin by sitting in silence. Reflect on your relationship with your parent. Review your reactions and behavior when interacting with them. Which of your reactions or behaviors is most uncomfortable for you? If you identify several, sort through them and select one.

You can complete the exercise for other troubling reactions at a later date.

2. After identifying your reaction or behavior, complete the following statement: "The reaction or behavior I want to change is . . ." Be very specific when completing this sentence. Try to identify a particular behavior associated with a troubling reaction and not just list the reaction.

3. Formulate a reasonable goal. That is, specify how you want to react or behave as a result of the desired change. Write down your goal ("My goal is to . . .").

4. The next step is to list all the strengths you have that could help you reach the goal. For example, you could list:

- I am a persistent person.

- I work hard to get what I want.

- I do not easily give up in the face of opposition.

   Be careful to keep the focus on you and not on how or what *you* can do to make the parent change.

5. List external constraints that could keep you from achieving your goal. The constraints can be people, events, conditions, and so on.

6. List internal constraints that may keep you from attaining your goal. How could you sabotage yourself?

7. Review all your lists. If your goal needs modification, this is the time to make the change.

8. On one three-by-five card, write the title, "I Can, I Will." Write all the strengths you identified under that title. Write the internal constraints on the other card giving it the title, "Do Not."

Put both cards in a wallet, purse, or some place where they are easily accessible. Review both lists at least once a week.

Do a goal check-up each month until you feel the change is entrenched and you don't have to think about what to do, you just do it. At this point you can tackle another desired change. Remember to be patient with yourself. It may take time to reach your goal.

Grounding Exercise 2: The Unexpected Act

Objective

The objective is to select a strategy to withstand an unexpected attack, accusation, or blaming from the destructive narcissistic parent. The mechanism you develop is temporary and will help contain triggered emotions until you are in a place where it is safe to examine them. As you become more adept at using the mechanism, you can move on to a more assertive stance.

Procedure

Sit in silence and recall the last time you interacted with your destructive narcissistic parent where you were unexpectedly and perhaps unfairly accused, blamed, or attacked. Do not revisit the emotions the incident brought up (hurt, resentment, etc.), and try not to dwell on the unfairness of the event.

Try and recall your posture, limbs placement, and what you think was your facial expression.

- Were you standing or sitting?

- Was the parent standing or sitting?

- Were others present?

- Where did it happen?

Was the behavior you remember typical for you and for your parent?

- Did you try to explain your position?

- Did you point out where they were in error?

- Did you contend that the accusation, blame, attack was unfair?

- Did you stay silent and obviously fume?

Once you establish to your satisfaction what happened and your verbal and nonverbal responses, imagine how you would feel if there had been a "wall of indifference" between the two of you when this happened. If you had been emotionally insulated from the hurtful remarks, allow yourself to imagine the relief you could feel. Keep this feeling, but put it aside for the time being and move on to the next step.

This part of the exercise needs practice, a mirror, and determination. It leads you through some grounding positions for unexpected attacks. All incorporate:

- placement

- body positioning

- limbs placement

- facial expression.

Placement refers to where you sit or stand in relation to the parent. Standing or sitting in front of them puts you in the "line of fire." It can also be a more aggressive position but if it hasn't helped to this point, you may wish to try a shift in placement. You can always return to what you are now doing.

Body positioning refers to the location and stance of your body relative to your parent.

- Are both of you standing or sitting, or is one or the other standing or sitting?

- Is your body turned toward them?

- Do you have a slight or profound forward lean toward them?

- Is your body relaxed or tense?

- Are your shoulders slumped or straight?

- Is your head turned toward them?

Limb placement means where your arms and legs are during the exchange. How are they placed? Are your arms crossed in front or behind you? Are they hanging down by your sides? Are your hands on your hips, clasped in front of you, or clenched in fists? Are you standing or sitting with your legs together? Crossed? Apart?

What facial expression do you have? Are you maintaining eye contact? Are you looking elsewhere (up, down, or to the side)? Are you frowning, smiling, or looking annoyed? Do you try to assume an expression of indifference? Ingratiation?

Once you have established what you physically look like and do during an exchange with the destructive narcissistic parent, you can practice assuming the following posture and expression in front of a mirror. Then, when you encounter an unexpected attack, you can remind yourself to assume these positions and expressions. It will become second nature to do so with time.

- **Placement:** Stand beside your parent when they sit or stand, either off to the side or slightly off to the side. Standing behind them is the best position, but probably will not be feasible.

- **Body positioning:** Turn your body away from the parent and lean back just a little. Consciously relax your shoulders and try to relax other parts of your body. Do not let your shoulders slump. If they do, straighten them but do not bring them too close to your ears.

- **Limb placement:** If standing, place your feet firmly on floor, nine to twelve inches apart. Let your arms hang loosely by your side, clasp your hands behind you, or cross your arms over your chest. Arms by your side without fists signals more relaxation, clasped behind you is "parade rest," and crossed in front of you signals defensiveness. Lots of options are available to you. If you want to be a little irritating and are wearing something with pockets, you can put your hands in the pockets and let your thumbs hang outside.

  If you're sitting, plant both feet on the floor, nine to twelve inches apart. Sit back and lean your head slightly back. Place your hands on your legs with fingers extended, or cross your arms over your chest.

- **Facial expression:** This will be the most difficult. Do not maintain eye contact. If you do look at them, do so briefly and then look away. Try for a neutral expression. Not exactly a "poker face," but one that sig-nifies polite indifference. Do not smile, frown, look hurt or annoyed.

The nonverbal positioning described can help insulate you from unexpected attacks, accusations, and blame. Used as a cluster of behaviors, they signal disinterest and indifference. Although this may not be the way you are feeling, using them can help prevent some of the parent's projections and projec-tive identifications from getting through to you. That alone will certainly help you cope. Some of your emotional intensity can be lowered and in time, some feelings will no longer be triggered at all.

Be patient with yourself. If you cannot do all of these strategies at once, do not give up. Continue to practice. Get so you can quickly assume your position so that the unexpected behavior does not fluster you. You can't always be on your guard, so there will continue to be times when your parent's unexpected behavior will be a surprise. Instead of giving in to the triggered emotions, concentrate on assuming your position.

Chapter 7

Becoming Aware and Making Conscious Choices

Awareness Expansion

Coping or dealing with unpleasant feelings triggered by your destructive narcissistic parent is not easy. Your feelings are deeply seated and the parent-child relationship contributes to the difficulty. This set of exercises is designed to help you learn new ways of coping but will not totally eliminate the unpleasant feelings generated in interactions with a destructive narcissistic parent.

These exercises will help you build, develop, and/or fortify your boundaries. You will explore your psychological, physical, and emotional boundaries and find where you can shore them up so as to become more separate and individualized, even if your parent tries to keep you from accomplishing this important developmental task.

The strength of your boundaries determines:

- how open you are to projections and projective identifications

- how you are able to handle rejection and hurt feelings

- what feelings are easily triggered in you.

Expanding your awareness of feelings also contributes to your development of healthy adult narcissism. You can become more open to experiencing a wide range of feelings rather than being restricted in the number and depth of feelings experienced. You can also increase your ability to be empathic. All these contribute to fostering the development and maintaining of satisfying personal relationships.

Awareness Exercise 1: The "Now" You

Objective

To assess the extent to which you perceive yourself as an adult

Time

At least one hour

Materials

Drawing materials for three pictures, writing materials

Procedure

Gather your materials and sit in a quiet place. Allow your thoughts to go back in time to when you were a child. As you reflect, if one event or image seems particularly important or meaningful for you, note that. If it involved your destructive narcissistic parent in any way, go to the next step. If it did not, continue reflecting until an image or event emerges that does involve the parent.

The next step is to draw an image or symbols for the event. Artistic talent is not important. Draw whatever appeals to you. For example, if the event was a conflict with the parent you could choose the parent's upset face, how you think your faced look, as some symbols for the conflict and feelings. After completing the picture, write "Child" at the top of a sheet of your writing paper and either write a brief description of the event or a list of feelings that you remember from that time and are re-experiencing now. Complete the following questions as if you were really in that time of your life.

I am now (age) _____ .

At this time I am _____ (try to stay in the present tense as if it were occurring now).

My parent _____ .

After this is complete, again sit in silence and recall your teen years. Recall an event with your parent when you were a teen. Draw and write about this event and answer the same three questions.

Return to sitting in silence and reflecting. This time concentrate on an experience you had with your parent since you either:

- reached the age of twenty-one

- finished your education or training

- moved out of the house

- became self-supporting

- got married

- became a parent.

Use any of these as your defining point for becoming and/or realizing you were (are) an adult. If none of these seem definitive for you, define it for yourself. If you find that you do not consider yourself as an adult, you will be using the information from your child and teen memories only.

Once you select your defining point for adulthood, allow an image to emerge of an interaction with your parent. Draw the picture and complete the writing as you did for the other two periods.

Take the pictures and place them side by side, considering how you depict yourself. What similarities do you see between how you stood, sat, held your body, and/or exhibited emotions on your face during the child and teen events and the "adult" event? Are you still physically orienting yourself to your parent as you did when you were younger?

Now review what you wrote and allow yourself to become aware of similarities in your feelings and responses for the three periods. Did you have similar answers for the sentences?

You have now reached the point where you can more easily see if you are continuing to relate to your parent as you did when you were younger, or if you have moved on to a more adult relationship with them. More than likely you have either not been allowed to move to a more adult relationship or you have not chosen to. It does make a difference which is the case for you, as it could be much harder to move into an adult relationship if your parent actively resists it. The awareness you get from completing this exercise can be a first step toward changing how you relate to your parent now that you are an adult.

Awareness Exercise 2: Focus on Positives

Objectives

To become more fully aware of inner resources that can be mobilized to better cope with the destructive narcissistic parent and to affirm strengths and accomplishments

Materials

Magazines and catalogues from which to cut pictures, scissors, glue sticks, several five-by-eight cards without lines, writing materials

Procedure

Gather all of your materials and sit at a table where you won't be disturbed. The task will be to construct three or more mini-collages. Each will relate to a characteristic selected from the following list and an achievement that illustrates that characteristic. First you will select a characteristic. Next, think of a personal achievement or accomplishment that required that characteristic. Write the name of the characteristic at the top of one of your cards and the achievement or accomplishment at the bottom.

Characteristics List

Determined	Optimistic
Persistent	Reliable
Goal-oriented	Resilient
Responsible	Caring
Independent	Rational

After selecting a characteristic and achievement, find pictures and symbols in your magazines that illustrate both, cut them out and paste them on the card. Repeat the procedure for at least two additional characteristics.

Place the collages side by side and really look at them. Write a brief response that completes the following sentence.

"When I look at my collages I am more aware and appreciative of my ability to . . ."

Write as much as you want. Construct a list of feelings that you experience as you review your collages. Then, go back and start a new card with a new characteristic.

The characteristics you're examining in this exercise are resources that you may be underusing but that are valuable. Do not forget them.

Awareness Exercise 3: Nonverbal Orientations

Objective

To become more aware of your consistent physical orientation to the destructive narcissistic parent

Materials

Photographs of you and others, of you and your parent, and of you and the other parent. Collect as many photographs for your different age levels as possible, including some current photographs. Candid shots may be more valuable sources of information but posed shots are also informative. Writing materials such as paper and pens.

Procedure

Gather materials and sit at a table in a quiet place. Organize the photographs by your age groups (child, teen, adult). You will work with each age group separately. Begin with the most current group of photographs. Lay them out in some order so that you can more easily see similarities and differences in your nonverbal orientations. "Orientation" refers to:

- distance between you and others in the picture

- degree of tenseness shown in your body

- positioning of arms and legs

- if you lean toward or away from others, especially your destructive narcissistic parent

- if the shot is candid, are you facing the parent of other person or are you turned away from them

- your facial expression

- hugs or other touches.

Record the similarities and differences you see in your orientation to your parent with DNP and that for others. Repeat the same process for the other two age groups.

Place what you've written for the three groups side by side. Observe and record the ways that you continue to orient yourself physically to your parent. Place a "C" beside those that were present in childhood and an "A" beside those that appear to have begun in adolescence.

Review all the recorded data and make a list of physical orientation behaviors with your parent that you want to adopt. Examples of physically orienting behaviors that you may want to adopt are: sitting slightly behind a parent, looking over the parent's shoulder when talking, raising your chin, and keeping a neutral facial expression. Examples of behaviors to change are: maintaining eye contact when talking, sitting, or standing face to face, and allowing your emotions to be easily shown on your face. Some readers may want to list the changes they would like to make, which can be helpful as a reminder not to do certain things. However, it is often more helpful to focus on what you want to do rather than what you don't want to do. Make both lists, if that appeals to you.

Awareness Exercise 4: Detoxifying

Objective

To develop your self by getting rid of some unpleasant feelings, and to emphasize a focus on positive feelings

Materials

A plain box, such as an inexpensive gift box, a purchased trinket box (at least four by six) that appeals to you, inexpensive paper in various colors, such as that used for copying. Get one sheet in as many different colors as you can. You can use plain, white paper also. Pen or pencil.

Procedures

Cut the paper in one-inch strips. If you are using colored paper, you will choose a color for different feelings as you go through the exercise (blue for sadness). Sit in silence and think of the feelings aroused in you by the acts and words of your destructive narcissistic parent. Do not obsess over these or allow the feelings to intensify. As you recall events, select a strip or strips of paper in the color that represents that feeling to you and write a word or two to describe one event and one of the feelings you experienced during that event. Put only one event and one feeling per strip. If you color-coded the emotions you may also want to give the emotion an intensity rating. For example, a fleeting resentment would get a 2 and a deep resentment a 9. Use a scale of 1 to 10, with 1 being mild and 10 the most intense.

As you complete a strip for each emotion in an event, put it in a pile. Try and keep the event piles separate. When you have strips for several events, sit back and look at your piles of strips. Note the array of colors for each and which colors seem to be repeated.

Take each pile and put them in the plain box, one at a time. Say out loud, "I am putting these unpleasant feelings about (name the event) away." When all the piles are in the box, put the top on and dispose of the box in one of the following ways:

- Open the box outside and toss the strips up, letting the wind disperse them. (Yes, this is littering.)

- Burn the box in the fireplace or a safe campfire.

- Dig a deep hole in your backyard or at a favorite outdoor spot and bury the box.

As you dispose of the box in the way that feels most powerful to you, concentrate on letting those feelings go. This symbolic purge can be much more effective than simply trying to convince yourself to not feel those old emotions any longer.

You may not be able to complete both parts of this exercise in one sitting but do not fail to do the next section at some point after the first part.

Exercise 4.2: Positives

Prepare strips of paper as you did in the first part of the exercise and sit in silence. Think of events where you had positive feelings. If there are some events with the destructive narcissistic parent that fall in this category, use them, but do not limit yourself to only events with that parent.

As you recall each event, write a one or two word descriptor on the strip and a feeling experienced. Limit each strip to one event and one feeling, rating for emotional intensity. Place the strips in separate event piles.

When you have completed strips for several events, look at your piles and the feelings experienced. Note if these piles are smaller than the ones for unpleasant feelings. If they are, consider how you can expand your range of pleasant feelings. You may also want to note whether the pleasant feelings are less intense than the unpleasant ones. This may also be something you can work to improve.

Place these strips in your "pretty" box and put them away. It could be helpful to put the box where you can see it and use it to remind yourself of pleasant feelings and the need to expand their frequency and intensity.

Making Conscious Choices

Characteristic of well-integrated individuals are their ability and willingness to make conscious choices. Children and immature adults do not make many conscious choices; they act on the basis of impulse, social and cultural convention, and parental messages. The difference for mature adults is that they carefully review all of these and then decide what, if any, they want to act on. They examine the options available to them and do not continue to consciously act in unproductive and self-defeating ways.

Many of your adult choices may be the result of lack of examination and conscious choice. For example, if you received a parental message that you were ineffectual and unable to succeed and are still fuming and acting on that message, then you may be engaging in self-defeating behavior that you need to discard.

The exercises that follow will guide you in examining what, if any, self-defeating and unproductive behavior you may have, especially any based on messages from the destructively narcissistic parent.

Choice Exercise 1:
Handling Conflicts with My Parent

Objective

To increase awareness of one's usual behavior in conflicts with parents and to create new and more satisfying ways to handle conflicts with parents

Materials

Two large sheets of newsprint, drawing materials, writing materials, desk

Time

At least one hour

Procedure

Go to a quiet place where you are not likely to be disturbed. Recall a continuing conflict with your parent or one that is still arousing significant distress for you. As you recall the conflict, make a list of all the feelings you remember having and those that still affect you as you think about conflict.

Use the drawing pens or pencils to give each feeling a color. Just draw a line beside the feeling with your color choice. Take one sheet of the newsprint and draw a shape to illustrate the most dominant feeling, using only the color you selected for that feeling. If the feeling was and is intense, make the shape large. If the feeling has moderated some, make the shape medium. Use a small shape for mild feelings or feelings that you think are gone. Look at what you drew and put it aside for now.

Using the same conflict, draw a scene from it that illustrates for you the essence of the conflict. The scene can be representational or nonrepresentational (a drawing of the setting of the conflict or just squiggles of color). Give your picture a title.

Place the two pictures side by side. Look at the feelings expressed by both. Then take a sheet of paper and put the feeling you've chosen at the top. List all of the associations you have for that feeling on a separate sheet. For example, if you listed "anger" at the top of the page, you might list associations like:

- Destructive

- Helpless

- Frighten

- Uncontrolled

- Ineffective

- Wrong

Do the same for two or three more feelings. Look at your lists and note commonalties. The commonalties point to a continuing underlying perspective that may be influencing your ability to constructively cope with feelings triggered by the parent. For example, if you feel helpless then you don't perceive that you can do anything that will make the situation more tolerable. Hence, you may have stopped trying without consciously deciding to do so.

Use the writing materials to record your answers to the questions using the assumption that your destructive narcissistic parent will continue to behave as they did in the conflict.

- What was said or done that triggered this feeling?

- What was the underlying message that was so upsetting? For example, was the message that I was inadequate now and forever?

- Did my response escalate the conflict and intensify my feeling?

- What else could I have said or done that might have been more effective?

- Could I have another response that would keep this feeling from being triggered?

It may not be possible to fully prevent future conflicts, but you can moderate their negative effects on you by changing how you respond. Since your parent is not likely to change and you want a different outcome, the most viable alternative is for you to change. You do not have to continue this pattern—you can choose to have a different response.

Choice Exercise 2: My Life's Course

Objective

To feel the course one's life has taken and to take stock of the current status of one's life

Materials

Large sheet of newsprint, eighteen by twenty-four or larger, pencil, felt markers in a variety of colors or crayons, two or three sheets of paper

Procedure

Find a table on which to work in a place that is as distraction-free as possible. Turn off the television. Soft music may be helpful to some people, but can be distraction for some. Select music that is calming and promotes reflection. Avoid loud, energizing music or that which is depressing or sad.

Sit in silence and let yourself reflect on your life. The memories and images do not have to emerge in chronological order, just let them come. Try to think of events, activities, and people from your preschool years, elementary school years, early adolescence, late adolescence, young adulthood, and present. Do not edit or change any of these—just let them come to you in any form.

On one sheet of paper, list the memories that present themselves to you. You could have categories already (elementary school years, high school) on the sheet prior to making your list so that you can record the memories in chronological order.

Draw the course of your life in the form of a lifeline on the newsprint. The course of your life should include and reflect at least ten of the events you remembered. You can use more of course, but try to use one or more from each period in your life. Select those that you feel are most important, significant, and/or changed the course of your life. Draw a symbol or picture to illustrate each event.

Use another sheet of paper to write a description of your life as it's depicted in the drawing. Then write a short description of the current period in your life—activities, relationships, level of satisfaction, and so on. You do not need to go into detail or explanations at this point; we will explore your current status in more depth in another exercise.

Processing

It would be helpful to write responses to the following:

- feelings experienced as you reflected on the course of your life and allowed memories to emerge

- significant events and people from your life that still have importance today

- feelings experienced as you drew your lifeline

- feelings experienced as you described your current status.

Choice Exercise 3: A Pictorial Self-History

Objective

To gain a perspective of the various stages of life one has experienced and to gain an appreciation of the various struggles, challenges, and accomplishments one has encountered

Materials

Four to six sheets of paper, each in a different color for periods in your life:

- childhood: before starting school

- childhood: ages six to twelve

- adolescence: ages thirteen to sixteen

- adolescence: ages seventeen to twenty

- early adulthood: ages twenty-one to twenty-eight

- adulthood: age twenty-nine on (these can also be divided in periods if you want)

Photographs of you and of significant others for each period, other mementos for each period. If you are using one sheet per period, it may be best to just use photographs. You will also need glue or double-sided tape to secure the photos.

Directions

Gather as many photographs and other mementos as you can before beginning to work. You may wish to obtain an attractive box in which to keep the materials, making it your "memory box." When you sit down to construct your pictorial history you may decide to do only one period at that sitting, divide the construction among several sittings, or do it all at once. However you choose to work, you will construct only one period at a time.

Sort through your photographs and select three to four you consider to be reflective of you during the particular period. Some people may choose to work from the present back to childhood, while others may prefer to begin with their childhood. You can also include pictures of significant others and events for each period. Whatever will fit on the page without making it too crowded will be effective. If you like, you could construct a collage of pictures, which will allow you to use more pictures on a page. Leave room at the top or bottom of the page for the title.

After placing and securing the pictures and mementos, sit back and reflect on your construction. Try to recapture feelings you experienced during that time. Give the period a name or title and record it on the page. Under the title write the sentence, "It was a period in my life when _____," and finished the thought. Do the same for each period.

Processing

Write a paragraph on a separate page about each period for which you constructed a pictorial history. You could use the following to begin your summary: "As I look at this pictorial history, I remember this part of my life as _____."

Choice Exercise 4: Parental Introductions

Objective

To understand how your parents' perspective of you differs from your self-perspective and to highlight any positive perspectives you and your parents have of you

Materials

Paper and pen or pencil. If you are keeping a journal, use that for writing.

Procedure

Sit in silence in a quiet place and close your eyes. Focus on your mother as she is, or as you imagine she would be, today and try to visualize her introducing you to a new acquaintance of hers. Open your eyes and write what you think she would say, the adjectives she would use, and the characteristics she would emphasize.

Repeat the procedure and visualize your mother talking about you to a relative. Write the details you imagine in this scenario.

Now repeat these visualizations for your father. Write these down also.

Now read your parental introductions. Allow yourself to become aware of any feelings you experience as you read these. List the feelings, as many as possible, and give each an intensity rating: "M" for mild, "O" for moderate, and "I" for intense. Next, rate each for pleasant ("P") or unpleasant ("U").

Processing

Write a summary statement or paragraph about how each parent introduces you, what the characteristics and adjectives chosen by them suggest about you, how consistent their perceptions of you are with your self-perceptions, and how the introductions make you feel about your parents and yourself.

Choice Exercise 5: Take Inventory

Objective

To highlight your current self-perception

Materials

A current photograph of you, a head-to-toe picture, pen or pencil, and paper

Procedure

Sit in silence and study your picture. Pay particular attention to your facial expression, pose, and posture. Try to remember what you were feeling and thinking when the picture was taken.

What does your photograph reveal about your current self? Do you see yourself as:

- happy or sad?

- confident or not-confident?

- tense or relaxed?

- satisfied or dissatisfied?

- comfortable or uncomfortable?

- serious or playful ?

- pleased or displeased?

What in your life was central for you when the picture was taken (work, career, family, a relationship, lack of a relationship, purpose or meaning in life, health concerns, financial concerns, and so on)? Write a brief statement about how this focus is reflected in your posture or facial expression.

You've worked through some or all of the exercises and now can begin to form a plan for action. Since it is unwise to try to make too many changes at once, take some time to reflect on what emerged for you from the material in the exercises. Your self-assessment of where and what you want to develop, where you have strengths that can be a considerable resource for changes, and priorities for change will contribute to your action plan. Begin with considering the theme that runs through what emerged in the exercises.

Which of the following could be the theme of your current status (your feelings about your life and your self):

- Lack of meaning or purpose in life

- Lack of a satisfying intimate relationship

- Problems in relationships with family or friends

- Problems with relationships at work, lack of self-confidence

- Feeling incompetent or flawed

- Lack of understanding and acceptance from others

- Feeling isolated and/or alienated

- Feeling overwhelmed by others' demands or expectations

- Feeling emotionally out of sync with others

- Insecure about your abilities to cope, be effective, etc.

- Hurt and angry at unfair blame, criticism, etc.

- Generalized dissatisfaction with self

- Current distressing interactions with parents

- Easily triggered guilt, shame

- Anger, frustration, hurt, rejection, resentment

- Incompetent, stupid

- Guilt for not meeting others' needs or expectations

It can also be helpful to try to do a self-assessment of your underdeveloped narcissism. That is, how you may be unaware of your grandiosity, sense of entitlement, lack of empathy, and so on. One of the most troubling aspects of underdeveloped and/or destructive narcissism is the person's inability to see those aspects of him or herself. Trying to take a self-appraisal can be difficult, but if you use criticisms others have of you to serve as a guide, you can increase your awareness of areas for development. Others in this instance do not include your self-absorbed parent(s).

Are you criticized frequently by others as:

- Overreacting

- Being detached or withdrawn

- Self-centered or selfish

- Insensitive

- Uncaring

- Expecting or demanding too much from others

- Insecure, unconfident

- Arrogant or cocky

- Overbearing

- Shallow

- Touchy or oversensitive to comments by others

- Considering yourself superior or inferior to others

- Being overly responsible

- Seeking the limelight, approval, etc.

It is now possible for you to have some goals and objectives for an action plan. Your self-reflection and self-assessment provided you with suggestions for changes and priorities for what to work on first.

An action plan would be similar to the following example.

My Action Plan

Goal

To decrease distressing interactions with my parent(s)

Objectives

Deploy emotional insulation prior to any interaction and use some nonverbal behaviors designed to reduce the parent's negative comments

Strategies

- Select my image for emotional insulation.

- Practice a conscious use of the image.

- Remember to deploy the image whenever I know I will have to interact with my parent(s).

- When my parent begins to criticize me, I will remove myself physically from their presence.

- If I cannot remove myself physically, I will "zone out."

- Another strategy will be to change the topic.

- When my parent begins to criticize me, I will stand or sit straighter, move my seat, and/or turn away from him or her.

As noted before, you will be much more successful if you select strategies in accord with your personality, with the understanding that you may still be unconsciously trying to please the parent. That is why it is also helpful for you to have an action plan to build, develop, and fortify your self.

Chapter 8

More Growth Strategies: Empathy

One characteristic of your destructive narcissistic parent that was, and still is, probably troubling to you is their lack of empathy. This parent can inflict considerable pain and, although you communicated the hurt both verbally and nonverbally, your parent doesn't seem to notice or care. This attitude and behavior adds insult to injury. How could he/she fail to notice or care?

Worse were probably the times when you tried to make your parent understand the impact of their words, attitudes, and/or behavior on you, but to no avail. Instead, they probably said you were just overreacting, out of line, ungrateful, or disrespectful. Not only did the parent not make any attempt to understand you, he/she blamed you for bringing the subject up, criticized you for daring to criticize him/her and most likely disparaged your feelings.

You may have continued to try to get through to them time and time again, but you weren't successful. No matter how many times you tried, whose advice you sought and took, or how you tried to model behavior by giving him/her what you wanted to receive, you were not successful. There may even have been instances where you felt you were making progress because the parent used some terms that seemed to indicate understanding. However, it did not take long before you realized that nothing had changed. The parent still didn't understand or seem to care.

Although your frustration continued (or continues) to grow, you still yearn for understanding and caring from that parent. It seems that no amount of evidence is sufficient to make you cease trying to get through to them. Your fantasy is alive and well.

While it would be advantageous (albeit very painful) for you to give up the fantasy, that's not what I'm proposing here. This discussion is not about how to get your parents(s) to change, it is about *your* growth and development in attaining empathy. You can keep your fantasy, but you can also do something about yourself to ensure that you do not end up lacking empathy.

Why You May Have Underdeveloped Empathy

You may not be as empathic as you think you are or as you want to be. You may not be as constricted as your destructive narcissistic parent is, but you may not have progressed very much.

When your destructively narcissistic parent did any of the following, your reaction (which may be unconscious) was to become wary of opening yourself up. Either that or you simply became enmeshed. Neither state is calculated to help develop empathy.

Did your parent:

- ridicule you

- show contempt for you

- make derisive comments to you or about you in your presence

- respond to you in a sarcastic way and/or make sarcastic remarks

- mock you

- act scornfully of you

- belittle your feelings and/or accomplishments

- stifle communication from you

- act arbitrarily and capriciously

- emotionally and/or physically abuse you

- insist that you conform to their expectations?

These are some of the conditions that can prevent a child from developing healthy boundaries, which are required in order to have real empathy.

Separation

Before beginning work on increasing and developing empathy, you need to examine your level and extent of separation and individuation. These are terms used to denote developmental processes that begin in childhood and continue through life. Individuation will be covered in the next section, but *separation* refers to having a clear psychic (internal image and understanding) representation of the self as different from everyone else, especially the mother. Most everyone achieves some degree of separation, but many continue to regard self as an extension of the mother. Some parents are not able to let their child be separate and continue to consider the child as an extension of themselves, beating back all attempts made by the child to become separate. This can be especially common in parents with a destructive narcissistic pattern, as they are often:

- overprotective

- smothering

- overly controlling

- manipulative

- prone to laying guilt trips.

Parents who act this way are desperately trying to keep their child from being separate. However, achieving a certain degree of separation is necessary for being empathic as an adult. Having a clear sense of where your "self" ends and "other" begins keeps you from becoming enmeshed or over-whelmed when you open yourself up to experiencing the other person's inner world— being empathic. If you don't have this clear psychic representation of self, you can find yourself taken over by the other person's feelings, wishes, desires, and fanta-sies, acting in accord with theirs instead of your own. Some theorists and authors refer to the state of being separate as maintaining boundaries. However, the development of strong, healthy boundaries is dependent on the degree and extent of separation that has been achieved.

Following is a short scale designed to provide an indica-tion of the extent to which you have progressed in the separa-tion process. Rate each item using the following:

5 - A great deal, almost always

4 - Considerable or often

3 - Sometimes

2 - Seldom, moderately

1 - Never, or almost never

Degree of Separation Scale

1. The extent to which you can say no to your parent and have few feelings of guilt.

2. The extent to which you can express disagreement with your parent.

3. The extent to which your feelings are respected by your parent.

4. The extent to which you can accept people who are different from you.

5. Your openness of emotional expression.

6. The extent to which you want, demand, or seek nurturance from family and friends.

7. The extent to which you want or demand friendship from those with whom you work.

8. The extent to which you subjugate your needs for those of others.

9. The lengths to which you will go to please others, try and make them happy, and so on.

10. The extent to which your parent's, spouse or lover's, and/or supervisor's disapproval upsets you.

11. The extent to which you seek external validation.

12. The extent to which you suppress unpleasant feelings.

13. The extent to which you fear rejection and abandonment.

14. The extent to which you can accept uncomfortable feelings.

15. The extent to which you yearn to have your destructively narcissistic parent meet your needs.

Scoring: The lower your score is, the more you have achieved psychological separation. Use the following as a guide.

60–75 Considerable enmeshment is present.

45–59 Some enmeshment is present; boundaries may be weak and/or fluid.

30–44 Progress has been made toward separation; boundaries are stronger.

15–29 Considerable progress has been made toward separation; strong boundaries.

0–15 Separation is almost complete.

Individuation

Individuation refers to identity formation. It is not sufficient to just separate—you also have to have a clear vision and understanding of who you are. It is also helpful to have freely and consciously chosen to be who you are rather than assuming beliefs, values, attitudes, and characteristics to please a parent

Reflect on exercise 7-10, where you listed significant events and decisions that shaped your life. How many of these were your conscious choice? Even as a child, were you allowed to make decisions or choices? Were you simply told what to do and be? As you look at yourself today, are your beliefs yours, or were they simply assumed and acted on? Do you have a clear idea of who you are?

The destructive narcissistic parent is unlikely to be of much assistance in helping their child achieve individuation. These parents tend to foster dependency and obedience to their demands and wishes, and to quickly stomp on any signs of resistance and rebellion. The child is not encouraged or allowed to make choices and decisions. This parent will use manipulation, emotional blackmail, distortions, lies, and even physical means to have the child do what the parent wants them to do.

Individuation Exercise 1: Define Yourself

Objective

To become aware of how you tend to categorize yourself and to highlight desired changes

Materials

Pen and paper

Procedure

Sit at a table or somewhere you can easily write. Without evaluating or editing your responses, write ten to twenty words and phrases to finish the sentence that begins with: "I am _____."

Have a minimum of ten endings and try to write twenty endings. Try not to read any further in this exercise before writing your responses.

When your list is complete, look at what you wrote and classify each response as a/an:

- Role

- Relationship

- External characteristic

- Internal characteristic

- Accomplishment

- Activity (like a hobby)

Reflection Questions

Did you have difficulty thinking of ten to twenty responses?

Did you change, edit, or eliminate something that came to mind? As you look at the responses and categories, which category has the most responses? The fewest responses? Which characteristics were chosen by you after careful consideration? Which were imposed by your parent(s) (excluding genetic characteristics)? Is this the "you" you want to be?

Becoming the "You" That You Want to Be

There are very few individuals who do not need to do more work on developing individuation. Indeed, this is a lifelong process, where progress can be made but the goal never completely achieved. This is due in part to external changes (economic and cultural) that come up and require that we reinvent or develop further our self-identity. Trauma and life circumstances like marriage, divorce, and children can also lead to questioning and changing the perception and answers to "Who am I?" In other words, you don't necessarily have to be the adult child of destructive narcissistic parent(s) to do this sort of self-examination.

How do you tackle such a big job? Well, you'll need courage, to be willing to take risks, and the willingness and ability to tolerate uncomfortable feelings—both your feelings and those of other people. My suggestion is to look at the following list of attitudes and behaviors and select the one or two you want to work on first without trying to make wholesale changes all at once. Trying to change everything now can be overwhelming and lead to discouragement when it doesn't work as planned. The list is divided into three categories: psychological and emotional, physical, and spiritual.

Psychological and Emotional

- Expressing your true feelings

- Allowing yourself to be aware of what you really feel

- Stating your preference for an activity (like what movie to watch)

- Not doing something just to please someone else

- Understanding and respecting your limits

- Developing hobbies and recreational interests

- Developing a network of social support

- Increasing your range of feeling expression (for example, by learning additional feeling words)

- Increasing your creativity at work, in your everyday tasks, and in any new activities you seek

Physical

- Taking good care of your physical self (sufficient sleep, nutritious meals, regular exercise)

- Learning to pay attention to your body

Spiritual

- Cultivating meaningful relationships

- Avoiding substituting chemicals or compulsions for being with yourself

- Reaching out and giving to others (volunteer work, mentoring, visiting)

- Taking time to meditate and center yourself

- Involving yourself in creative endeavors

- Examining your values: keeping those that you freely choose, discarding the others or those that are no longer relevant

During the period when you strengthen your boundaries by completing more of the developmental tasks of separating and individuating, you can also begin to work to reduce empathic failures and increase empathic responding. Notice that I did not say to increase being empathic. Empathy, as used in this discussion, is a state of being—not just a set of skills. Skills are important and can be taught. Being, as a state, cannot be taught—it is achieved. Your desire to become more empathic, your fostering of healthy narcissism, and developing your empathy skills should all result in your becoming more empathic.

This section will emphasize strategies and techniques you can use that will:

- help you tune in to what the speaker may be feeling

- keep you in touch with what you are thinking and feeling

- extend your range of feeling responses

- show you how to paraphrase and reflect what the speaker is saying and feeling

- teach you to observe nonverbal behaviors that help identify what the speaker may be feeling

- describe behaviors and responses that are indicative of empathic failures.

Empathic Failures

Although it may be more profitable to build on strengths rather than to work on deficiencies, it can be very helpful to begin this discussion by looking at empathic failures. That is, to describe some behaviors—both verbal and nonverbal—that signal empathic failure. The result in failing to be empathic with someone is that they then often feel:

- devalued

- unimportant

- unappreciated

- unloved

- misunderstood

- not cared for

- dismissed.

Not everyone will feel all of these all of the time. But all you have to do is to reflect on how you felt, or feel, when your destructive narcissistic parent fails to have empathy for you to get a deep understanding of the impact of your empathic failures on others. Even if you feel you're an empathic person, you may be surprised at how often you fail to demonstrate real empathy.

To give you an idea of how often empathic failures can occur, even with well-meaning people, consider the following examples. Read them and reflect on how often you do any of them when someone is talking to you.

- Allow your attention to drift to other concerns, people, chores, and so on

- Become bored

- Abruptly change the topic with or without notice

- Ask questions (some questions may be necessary for adequate information but too many times questions are asked when further information is not needed)

- Gaze around the room or in the distance

- Abruptly break off the conversation

- Turn your body away from the person

- Cross your arms over your chest

- Lean backwards from the person

- Think about personal concerns while the person is talking

- Mentally criticize the person who is talking

- Mentally phrase your response

- Interrupt the speaker

- Distract them in some way (like straightening their collar).

Most people do some of these frequently. Not always, but enough so that they are engaging in empathic failures more often than they think.

Empathic failures can be repaired. The ideal, of course, is to not fail empathetically—to make an empathic response. But almost as good is to catch yourself in the midst of an empathic failure and turn your attention to the person speaking to you. Acceptable is to acknowledge your failure later, apologize, and try to atone. An example for each follows.

Immediate Repair

You are in a conversation with a friend at lunch where she is telling you about an incident with a coworker that was upsetting. You are only halfway listening to her, mainly thinking about what you will wear to a party that evening. You make soothing comments to your friend.

This is an empathic failure you could immediately repair. You must first become aware that you are, indeed, failing to be empathic with your friend. Soothing comments do not acknowledge the friend's feelings, they only serve to convey that you do not want the friend to feel as they do. Thinking about your future concerns means that you are not being present and focused on the speaker. Both are conditions needed for you to be empathic.

Once you accept that you're not being empathic with your friend, you can immediately bring your attention to her, reflect some of her feelings (see next section on making empathic responses), and stay more present while you listen.

Delayed Response

Let's suppose that it is only when you're having your morning coffee the next day that you realize that you were not empathic. You may even feel guilty or ashamed for being preoccupied with personal concerns and, in effect, minimizing something your friend considered important.

You can repair the empathic failure now. "Repair" in the sense that you acknowledge to your friend that you really didn't give her the attention she merited, and you want her to know that you did hear her, even if your responses did not adequately convey that. "Hear" is used in the sense to mean that you understood what feelings were expressed and/or meant. You can go on to label or identify the feelings so that you're not just giving lip service to understanding. You still don't have any answers or solutions, but you have now let your friend know that you did hear her feelings. This simple repair work can strengthen a relationship and promote trust.

The delayed response is not ideal, but it's infinitely better than continuing to let the empathic failure stand. This is especially true with children, who can be more forgiving than adults. If you have never tried to repair empathic failures with a child, try doing so and notice the direct and indirect payoffs. You are demonstrating to the child that you:

- care about him/her
- understand what they are feeling
- can admit to making a mistake
- are willing to try to make amends.

You may be pleasantly surprised at how positively even teens will react to your attempt to repair empathic failures.

Increasing Empathic Responses

So far, our focus has been on building psychological boundaries to increase the emotional and unconscious understanding of where you end and others begin and to reduce or eliminate empathic failures. But two other items are basic to empathy:

being empathic and increasing empathic responses. Once some measure of both of these are in place, it becomes easier to respond with empathy.

You now know that some of your usual responses that:

- question

- soothe

- deflect

- distract

- challenge

- intellectualize

- try to "solve"

- become personal.

while intended to show empathy or understanding, will fall short of the mark. You may also have increased your awareness of nonverbal behaviors that contribute to reduction or absence of empathy. These behaviors fall in the categories of not physically, emotionally, or cognitively (consciously) attending to the speaker. Since these behaviors carry the major portion of any message you send out to others, the discussion begins with them.

Nonverbal Responses

Nonverbal communication carries the "real message," the emotional and/or unconscious meaning or intent. This means that you may be unaware of the message your body position, eyes, facial expression, and tone of voice are conveying to the other person. And, while the other person is reading and reacting to the real message on mostly an unconscious level, the verbal and conscious portion of the message is much less important. When the verbal and nonverbal messages are in conflict, the nonverbal message takes priority. This is one of the primary reasons we're starting with nonverbal behavior Begin by becoming aware of your:

- body position and orientation

- facial expression

- arm and leg positioning

- eye contact

- voice tone

when you are talking with someone who is important to you. Once you can tune in to what you're currently experiencing (and this may take some time, so be patient), change what you're doing so that:

- your body is oriented to the speaker

- you make eye contact and sustain it to the extent that you and the other person are comfortable

- slightly lean forward to the other person

- place your arms and legs in an open, relaxed position

- make a habit of sitting and standing directly to the speaker whenever possible. At least do not turn your body away from the speaker.

Sustained eye contact can be intimidating to some and too intimate for others. However, maintaining eye contact conveys interest and, in some cases, it conveys caring. Try not to put your focus on the center of the person's forehead, the nose, or slightly off from the person's eyes. That behavior is more off-putting than looking away from the person. Practice until you can be comfortable maintaining eye contact throughout the entire conversation.

Lean toward the speaker. Not too much as this may make them feel you are invading their space, using your body to intimidate or manipulate, or are introducing too much intimacy. That would be counterproductive. Slightly leaning forward is helpful in making the person feel you are interested in them.

An open, relaxed position indicates that you're receptive, willing to listen, and ready to give and receive trust. Do not cross your arms and/or legs, clench your fingers, fidget or make other nervous mannerisms, jiggle objects, stroke hair or other body parts, fiddle with jewelry or coins in a pocket. All of these are distracting gestures that convey inattention and/or distractions.

Your tone of voice carries considerable information about your feelings—much more so than the actual words used. When working on increasing your empathic responses, pay attention to how your voice sounds and take steps to soften your tone, slow the pace of your speech, and pause briefly before responding.

Avoiding Some Common Traps

There are some behaviors and attitudes to avoid if you want to increase your empathic responding. But first, you must become aware of whether you engage in any of the following:

- interrupting the speaker
- finishing the speaker's thought or sentence
- asking questions instead of making statements
- turning the topic to you and your personal story or concerns
- becoming defensive, angry, or emotionally intense
- telling the person what he/she should or ought to do or think
- challenging the speaker's feelings.

Interrupting the speaker can be disconcerting, causing the person to lose their train of thought and/or leading to the belief you're not interested in him/her or what he/she is trying to say. For some people, interruptions are considered rude and may cause them to be less forthcoming to you.

Finishing the speaker's thoughts or sentence is similar to interrupting the speaker. It differs in that you are using your words, projections, and thoughts and not giving the speaker time and space to complete what they were saying.

Asking questions can be very counterproductive, although many people think they're trying to show interest when asking questions. However, asking questions can have the opposite effect, as some people feel attacked or assaulted when several questions are asked. This can be especially true when they're asked numerous questions in succession. Another disadvantage to asking questions is that those questions are often really rhetorical and making a statement would be more positive. Try making a statement every time you start to ask a question and notice how often you could be a more effective communicator by restricting your questioning behavior.

I'll bet that one of the behaviors of your destructive narcissistic parent(s) that irritates you is how frequently the conversation is turned to his/her personal concerns. What can be sobering is to examine your own behavior and notice how often you do the same thing when talking with others. You may think that what you're doing is intended to connect with the speaker and show that you understand, but what comes across is that you are much more interested in your personal concerns than you are in what the speaker is talking about.

Another trap to avoid is becoming defensive or emotionally intense, which reduces or eliminates your capacity to tune in to what the other person is saying, feeling, and meaning. You become more focused and concerned about protecting and defending yourself, so immersed in your emotions that the other person's communication is easily distorted or not heard at all. This is another reason why it's so important that you learn to tune in to what you are feeling and accurately gauge its intensity so that you can be much more aware when your defenses and emotions are such that the speaker's message is apt to be distorted.

Giving advice and/or telling the speaker what they should or ought to do is also counterproductive in most instances. This is the case even when they ask for advice, as you are not the same as the speaker nor can you fully understand their needs, desires, or circumstances. While it can be tempting to try to fix the problem, there are more constructive ways than offering advice to accomplish that objective. You may have some information that could be helpful and welcome, but telling someone what they *should* or *ought* to do does not fall in that category. It's also much more constructive and helpful when interacting with children or teens to make it clear when you're giving an order. It can be confusing when your communication is disguised by using "shoulds" and "oughts." Those terms can make it appear that the other person has some small choice available. Thus, children and teens may take advantage of the small opening or be paralyzed by indecision as to what your real intent is.

When you challenge someone's feelings, you are, in an indirect, disguised way, saying that the feelings are wrong or inappropriate. It is possible that the other person is overreacting, or are reacting to old parental messages instead of objective reality, and that is what's contributing to the seemingly off-target feeling. However, this is their feeling, they are entitled to the feelings, and you do not help the communication between you by challenging them. A challenge is much more likely to have an unintended result, making the other person defend, counterattack, or withdraw from the communication and relationship.

Identifying Empathic Responses

Following are two exercises to practice identifying empathic responses. Empathic responses are those that speak to the dominant or complex feelings underlying what the speaker says. An empathic response does not:

- extend what the speaker says

- focus only on content

- express the listener's thoughts or feelings

- request more information

- engage defenses

- demean or devalue the speaker

- show the listener's superiority.

The first scale presents some situations and four or five possible responses. Assume you are the listener and select the response you feel comes closest to being empathic. Each situation will have an empathic response. The listener is indicated in bold print.

Identification of Empathic Responses

1. Teenage girl to **mother**: "Get off my back!"

   a. "I'm your mother. Don't talk to me like that."

   b. "I'm only trying to do what's best for you."

   c. "I know you want to decide things for yourself."

   d. "I'm not on your back. I'm just making a suggestion."

   e. "It irritates you when you think I'm trying to tell you what to do."

2. Wife to **husband**: "You're always off to something after work and on weekends. If it isn't Little League or meetings at your clubs, you're over to Bob's house."

   a. "What do you mean by 'always off'? I spend plenty of time at home."

   b. "You're annoyed that I seem to spend more time away than here."

   c. "I'm just trying to do what I feel is right for the kids and the community."

   d. "You know Bob is having a hard time with his illness and all. You ought to feel more understanding."

   e. "Get off my back."

3. Woman to **friend**: "I have so much to do, I don't know where to start."

   a. "You can get overwhelmed when a lot is expected of you."

   b. "It feels like you need some time off."

   c. "I'm getting tired just hearing all you have to do."

d. "Have you thought about getting some outside help?"

e. "Don't take so much on yourself. Give some of the work to others."

4. Student to **teacher**: "Do I have to study for this test?"

a. "Do you want to pass the course?"

b. "Of course you have to study for the test."

c. "You're asking me if you have to study? Don't you know what you need to do?"

d. "You have a lot to do and studying for a test seems overwhelming."

e. "You're hoping you can get by without having to study for this test."

5. Man to **boss**: "Evan is a goof-off. He's always trying to load his work onto me. I'm sick and tired of it."

a. "You wonder if your efforts are appreciated."

b. "Tell me more about Evan and his behavior of putting work on you."

c. "You need to focus on your work more. Forget about Evan."

d. "What can I do to help?"

e. "You're just envious of Evan."

The correct answers are: 1. c, 2. b, 3. a, 4. d., 5. a. You may have already noticed, that all of the incorrect choices fell into one or more of the following categories:

- asking questions
- giving advice
- asking for more information
- trying to "fix it"
- accusations.

There are times and circumstances where the incorrect answers are appropriate, but they still aren't empathic and the real goal here is to increase your empathic responding.

Let's practice more empathic responses with two of the scenes from the scale.

1. Woman to **friend**: "I have so much to do, I don't know where to start."

What feelings might she be experiencing? List all you can think will fit.

2. Student to **teacher**: "Do I have to study for this test?"

What feelings might the student be feeling? Again, list all you can think of.

To make an empathic response, select one feeling for each situation and put it in a sentence ("You're feeling _____"). Try to curb any tendency or inclination to remind the student or friend of their responsibility, give a sarcastic response, or moralize in any way. None of those would be empathic.

As you practice focusing on and expressing feelings you will find more and better ways of making empathic responses. Starting out with "You feel _____." helps remind you to focus on their feelings, or what you think they are feeling. This is a good beginning.

The second scale we'll work with gives you practice in developing empathic responses. For each of the scenes, first make a list of feelings you think could be those of the speaker. Then construct a response using one or more of those words. The listener is in bold.

1. Man to **wife**: "I want to watch the ball games this afternoon. Will your mother be coming over?"

Feelings: _____

Response: _____

2. Child to **parent**: "No. I don't want to go to grandma's house."

Feelings: _____

Response: _____

3. Boss to **secretary**: "Where in the hell are those bro-
chures? The printer was supposed to deliver them
yesterday."

Feelings: _____

Response: _____

4. Committee member to **Chair**: "Shouldn't we take a
vote before doing anything?"

Feelings: _____

Response: _____

5. Friend to **friend**: "You told my secret to Jane. I asked
you to keep it confidential and you didn't."

Feelings: _____

Response: _____

Match your response to examples below. You may have
selected different feelings from those in the example, but the
essential format should be the same.

1. You are hoping to have a quiet afternoon.

2. You're feeling trapped into doing something you don't
want to do.

3. It's annoying when other people don't meet their
responsibilities.

4. You are feeling some ambivalence about what's being
proposed.

5. You're hurt and feeling betrayed because you think I
told Jane your secret.

The essential component for making empathic responses
is that you have to get out of yourself. Your focus must be on
the other person. However, it is unrealistic and perhaps
unwise to try and be empathic with everyone all of the time.
Restrict the major part of your empathy to those people who
are most important to you. Above all, do not try to be
empathic with someone who has a destructive narcissistic pattern. They will eat it up—trying to swallow you in the process.

Chapter 9

Building Humor and Creativity

Can you be silly? Do you see the absurdities in your thoughts, behaviors, or attitudes, and can you laugh at them? Do you laugh at puns, shaggy dog stories, childish jokes, and limericks? What makes you laugh, snicker, or chuckle?

Humor, like so many other things, is very individualistic. That is, the same thing is not funny to everyone. But humor is a characteristic of healthy adult narcissism, and in this chapter you'll begin exploring how you respond to humor.

Hurtful Humor

I think it's important to distinguish between healthy humor and hurtful humor, for hurtful humor is to be avoided and is not a characteristic of healthy adult narcissism. Hurtful humor is really masked or disguised anger, hostility, or sadism, with the goal of getting revenge. The revenge is not necessarily against the present target of the humor, but instead can act as "payback" for a lifetime of real or imagined wounding. The attitude of someone who uses hurtful humor is, "Someone really hurt me, and I cannot retaliate for one reason or the other, so I'll retaliate against others who present themselves." The person using harmful humor also is reluctant to accept responsibility for being wounding, so they use humor to cover it up or to provide an escape if detected by the target. Some forms of harmful humor are:

- sarcasm

- put-downs

- ridicule

- racial/ethnic jokes

- gender jokes

- jokes that poke fun at disabilities

- tickling

- practical jokes.

These acts can demean and wound while giving the initiator a cover so he/she can say that they were "only joking." Our culture demands that we be able to "take a joke" and minimize its impact on us. It is very difficult to go against a cultural or social norm and admit that you didn't see the humor in a joke, or that you were offended or wounded.

Your Best Defenses

What is a good or helpful response to hurtful humor? After all, your destructively narcissistic parent may use you as the target of their hurtful humor, which is not humor at all but just another way to belittle, demean, and devalue you. You may have experienced this action for years, but their hurtful humor still has considerable power to wound you. Strategies to defend against or eliminate hurtful humor directed your way are:

- stop joining in the mirth

- define new limits

- fog and frustrate

- appear to agree.

Refuse to Join in the Mirth

The first most effective strategy is to stop laughing or smiling when a joke is told that makes you uncomfortable. As a matter of fact, you may want to practice this in every facet of your life, not just with the parent with a DNP. Stop laughing at comments, remarks, stories, and jokes that put others at a disadvantage because of a characteristic, such as race or gender. When such jokes are made in your presence, do not laugh.

The second step, used in combination with step one, is to say clearly that you don't see the humor in the joke. You do not have to be combative, angry, defiant, or attacking when saying this. You can simply be matter of fact. Phrases such as:

- "I missed your point."

- "That was not funny."

- "I don't see what's funny about that."

These and other such phrases can be very effective. If challenged, a quiet shrug and comment that humor is subjective will stop any challenge. Someone will change the conversation to a less sensitive topic.

If you have laughed in the past with the destructive narcissistic parent when he/she makes ridiculing comments about you, the first step is to stop smiling or laughing when the parent makes those remarks now. Do not protest or challenge, as this will not be effective. Just don't join them in demeaning yourself. A quiet rebellion will work well. You do not need to say that:

- you disagree

- you are hurt by the remarks

- the parent is being mean and insensitive

- the parent should be making confidence-building remarks.

You simply give the remarks a cold shoulder and move on.

Define New Limits

Another strategy would be to define some new limits for what you are willing to accept. When the parent makes a ridiculing remark, you could say something like, "Making slighting remarks about me is not funny." Be prepared for the reaction that you "can't take a joke," that you're being oversensitive, or some other reaction that is intended to place you in the wrong. Stick to your guns and deal with any triggered feelings later.

Fog and Frustrate

Fogging and frustrating is always effective if you can detach yourself from the emotional content and reaction. When you use this strategy you diffuse the person's intent by asking questions that will point out the absurdity of what they've said. For example, if a parent were to tell you that you looked frumpy, you could ask a series of questions such as:

- "What about me is the frumpiest?"
- "Is there anything else that is frumpy?"
- "How do you define frumpy?"
- "Can the frumpiness be rescued?"
- "Frumpy is wrong? How so?"

With practice you can become adept at asking a series of questions that will illuminate the real meaning of a nasty joke, fogging and frustrating the joker's intentions.

Appear to Agree

The final strategy presented is to appear to agree. This may be perceived as sarcasm but does not have to be. To illustrate, in the previous example you could appear to agree with the comment about looking frumpy by saying, "I certainly hope so. After all, that's what I was trying to do." Or, "It's the 'in' thing now."

I've used this strategy when someone tells me I look tired. My response is, "I hope so, since I am tired." Or, "I'd hate to be tired and not look it."

Healthy Humor

There are many benefits to healthy humor, both physical and psychological. You will want to develop this aspect of yourself for more reasons than just developing healthy narcissism.

Physical benefits revolve around strengthening your immune system, which makes you more resistant to disease and better able to cope with stress and stress-related diseases. Stress- related diseases, such as hypertension, heart disease, and gastrointestinal distress, are shown by empirical studies to be helped by the preventive and healing effect of laughter (Hafen et al. 1996).

There are many psychological benefits to humor according to Hafen, and all of these will enable you to better cope with your destructively narcissistic parent.

Constructive uses of humor can:

- improve your negotiating and decision-making skills
- help maintain a personal sense of balance
- improve your performance
- empower you
- relieve stress
- improve your ability to cope with everyday stress and difficult people
- promote creativity.

How can you develop healthy humor? First, take an inventory of where you are in the world of humor. Assess the frequency with which you engage in the following activities using the rating scale.

Your Humor Status Scale

5 – Everyday   2 – More than once a month

4 – Two or more times a week   1 – Less than once a month

3 – At least once a week

1. Laugh out loud several times

2. Say something that makes someone laugh

3. Do something silly

4. Read the comics in the newspaper

5. Watch cartoons on TV

6. Attend a funny movie or play

7. Find something to add to my humor collection

8. Read and/or buy a humorous book

9. Rent funny movies

10. Look for the humor in my predicaments

Scoring

40–50   You are well on your way to developing healthy humor.

30–39   You can find humor, but you could develop it further.

20–29   You laugh occasionally, but there is not much merriment in your life.

below 20   Get to work *now!*

Even if you are well developed in healthy humor, you may want to explore some of the suggestions for increasing humor. They're just plain fun.

Make a commitment to laugh out loud several times a day. Instead of smiling at something, try laughing with pleasure. Laughing does not take long—it can be only a few seconds in duration. But during that time, you can lift your (and others') spirits.

Do something silly every day. I mean "silly" in the sense that you don't expect to find an adult doing whatever it is. It doesn't have to be stupid, just kinda goofy. Things you remember doing in childhood could suffice. For example:

- spin around in a circle with your arms out and laugh

- skip instead of walking for a short distance

- when drinking a soda alone, make bubbles by blowing air through the straw

- take a bath, put your head under the water, and blow bubbles

- wear a silly hat

- recite passages from Dr. Suess's books to someone

- dance all by yourself.

Personally, I think reading from Dr. Suess is an especially wonderful experience. For some reason, the character *The Cat in the Hat* was being talked about in one of my graduate classes. Someone mentioned *Green Eggs and Ham* and, since I had memorized parts of it, I began to recite it. I went on from there to recite parts of *One Fish, Two Fish*. By the time I finished, the class was positively gleeful, laughing and applauding. We all felt better after that interlude.

A side benefit for engaging in humor daily is that you will be able to avoid "sweating the small stuff," distinguishing the important from the unimportant. Lightening up and finding the humor makes you and everyone around you feel better.

Creativity

Creativity is an essential component of healthy adult narcissism. However, many people have a narrow definition of creativity. What comes to mind when you think about creativity? Do you consider creative works and endeavors to be limited to "artists," such as musicians, painters, sculptors, and so on? Does the person or work have to be recognized or proclaimed as "creative" by experts in the area? If any of these constitute a part of your perception of creativity, you're probably taking a much too narrow view. Creativity is a much broader concept, especially as a characteristic of healthy adult narcissism.

Many of the people who've been considered creative through the ages would not be considered as having healthy adult narcissism when their behavior and relationships are reviewed. Many famous people who produced creative works also exhibited destructive or pathological narcissism.

Our discussion of creativity will focus on a broader definition that includes originality, expressiveness, and imaginative spirit in:

- making

- producing

- designing

- inventing

- discovering

products, processes, and procedures. This definition allows for a wider array of creativity and holds out the promise that everyone can develop the creativity they need for healthy adult narcissism. You don't have to be an "artist," nor be recognized by anyone as creative, nor produce something for display and criticism. You can be creative in that way, or in many other ways.

Originality means new or novel. That is, much of what you do in producing uses existing or available materials, or techniques in a different way. It does not necessarily mean that you were the first to do so—that is unlikely. It does mean that, for your purpose, in your environment, you put it together in a new way.

Imaginative means that you thought it out, extended the known and existing boundaries, and/or used nonlinear thinking to be original. You were not constrained by convention, conventional thought and wisdom, or personal constraints, like wanting to conform. You explored "What if?" and found that you could visualize a way to accomplish whatever it was you were working on.

Expressiveness means that you expressed your creative impulse in some way. You created and produced a product, a performance, a process, or other outcome—there was some tangible communication of your creation.

Nonlinear or "Outside the Box"

A science-fiction book series in the 1960s had an underlying theme around non-Aristotelian thinking, or "null A," taken from the field of general semantics (Korzybski 1933). The contention was that current Western thought was Aristotelian ("if this is true, then that is true"), which was limiting to thought and creativity. Aristotelian logic is deductive, not intuitive, and relies heavily on experimentation. Characters in the book who were taught "null A" were able to be more effective, creative, and productive, as they weren't bound by having to follow a preconceived set of procedures, ideas, or notions. They could proceed in any direction.

This "null A" thinking is a good example of nonlinear or "outside the box" thinking and doing. The possibilities for everything are infinitely more vast than when only linear and conventional thinking and doing are used. Trying to think in a less conventional, less ordinary way is what I think of as creativity. Thinking of it in this way expands and enhances the common perception of creativity, taking it out of the realm of only a few talented people and making it an option for almost everyone.

Building Your Creativity

How would you rate yourself on creativity? Use a scale of 1 to 10, with 10 being very creative, and give yourself a rating. Record your rating on a sheet of paper and keep it. We'll be using it later.

When thinking about developing your creativity there are some internal states that you should pay special attention to, such as:

- awareness
- spontaneity
- wonder

- intuition

- sense of adventure.

Read the descriptions of these states that follow and evaluate how developed that state is for you and how much you think you can develop each particular state. The best places where you can begin to make changes are your everyday life, hobbies, and work activities. Use all three or any others that you desire. We are beginning to work outside the box.

The first state is the level of your awareness of who, what, and "when" you are. To what extent do you experience the world in the here and now? Are you aware of your sensations at all times, or do you have to concentrate? Are you constantly thinking about the past or future, or can you be centered in the present? The aware person is one who stays in touch with what he/she is seeing, hearing, feeling, tasting, and smelling at all times. This person is in tune to what their body is telling them and, at the same time, what messages the external world is sending.

The second state is your degree of spontaneity. Can you be spontaneous, or do you carefully consider what to do, think, or feel before experiencing? Spontaneity does not mean responding to foolish impulses. Adults who are in touch with reality will not be impulsive, as this can lead to sometimes fatal errors in judgment. Spontaneity means that you can explore new ways of thinking, feeling, and responding; be in the moment; and understand that freedom also means responsibility. You can spontaneously laugh, cry, move, and be at one with the universe.

Wonder is the third state to consider. I think of wonder as an openness to experiencing. Think of children and how everything is a wonder to them as they encounter it for the first time. They become transfixed, examine the new thing or situation in amazement, and remain open in their reaction. In the adult, wonder can be similar. You would dream up new ways of perceiving and doing just about everything and be captivated by the uniqueness and beauty of your world. You would look for wonder every day and all around you.

The fourth state is intuition. This state uses inductive reasoning, hunches, flights of fancy, and imagination. You don't have to wait for all the information to come in as you realize that you may never gather enough information to prevent errors or to have certainty. Suddenly, seemingly out of the blue, using a process you cannot explain, you can see the relationships, extend the possibilities, work through the problem, and formulate a solution. When this happens, you're using your intuition. Insight and intuition can work together to produce an outcome quickly. Do you trust your intuition? Or does your desire for certainty make you wary of what your intuition is telling you?

Adventurousness is the last state. Are you willing to take some psychological risks? Do you fear failure to the point where you're unwilling to try anything new, different, or where you might make a mistake? Do you fear that others will ridicule your efforts? There may be past experiences that contribute to a lack of being adventurous. These will have to be worked through and accepted so that you can once again take the risk of doing something untried, rebound from any failures, and try once again. You may not succeed, but if you do not try you're guaranteed not to succeed. On the other hand, you can gain much from just making the attempt.

How did you rate yourself on each of the states? Which state(s) could use the most development? Have you discovered some blocks to your creativity such as:

- fearing to be thought foolish

- feeling incompetent or inept

- worrying about what others may think

- expecting ridicule or other judgments

- needing certainty about how to proceed and what to expect

- thinking there is a "right" way

- feeling uncertain about how and where to begin?

You are not alone. Many people who could unleash and express their creative sides are constrained by similar thoughts, attitudes, old parental messages, and past experiences. It's not easy to get beyond these, but it can be done.

How You Rated Yourself

Go back to your self-rating of creativity and look at the rating. Unless you rated yourself a 7 or above, you may have underestimated your creative self. How so? If you worked through the exercises presented in this book, you have expressed your thoughts, feelings, and ideas in new and novel ways for you. These are exercises that used art, writing, movement, and images and many of them may have made you stretch your creative muscles.

This brings up a very important point about creativity. You can feel free to create just for creativity's sake. Create for yourself, not for external acclaim or recognition. The reward is in the process of expressing important personal perceptions. And this brings up the second important point I'd like to stress: that creativity is a process—not the product or outcome. The enjoyment, pleasure, and satisfaction of creativity emerges during the process. There certainly can be some or all of these reactions when looking at the outcome, but the process is where you can "lose yourself," "zone out," and experience the creative endeavor.

When you did the exercises earlier in the book did you become:

- immersed

- interested

- excited

- surprised

- invested?

Did you:

- attain new insights and understandings

- gain another perspective

- feel pleasure

- make a vow or commitment?

All of these results were possible and represent examples of what the creative process feels like. After considering just how creative you've been in working with this book, you may have to reconsider how creative you are.

Getting Started

There are other ways to build and develop your creativity and each person has to establish their own personal approach. What works and is satisfying for one person may not fit anyone else. You certainly don't have to follow someone else's approach to developing your creativity, and even if you choose to begin that way, you are free to let your own style evolve.

Following are some activities that can help you jump into creative endeavors. Feel free to modify them to appeal to you. There are a variety of activities, but these are only a few of the vast array possible. They are presented for enjoyment and creativity- building only and are not used for guided self-exploration.

Creativity Exercise 1: Patterns

Objective

To practice being spontaneous and creative

Materials

White three-by-five or four-by-five notepad, black doodle pad the same size, writing pencil(s) or drawing pencil(s), either a white drawing pencil, white crayon, white oil pastel, or white gel pen, tape

Optional Materials

Three three-by-five or four-by-six pieces of stiff paper, like poster board.

Directions

Sit at a well-lit table in a comfortable chair. Pretend you have been asked by a designer to produce as many different black-and-white patterns as you can for costumes to be worn at a very posh event. People attending the event cannot wear only black or only white, they must wear a combination. You will be paid handsomely for every different black-and-white pattern you create.

Use the pencils on white paper and your choice of white markers on the black paper. Allow fifteen minutes for the first series. Draw as many different black and white patterns as you can during this period, using one piece of paper for each design.

At the end of fifteen minutes, stop. Spread all your designs out on the table and review what you produced. You may want to organize them, such as putting all the designs with circles together. Take some time to examine your designs, visualizing them as designs for costumes.

As you look at your designs, you may begin to think of other patterns not drawn. Return to your materials and draw new patterns for ten minutes. At the end of that time, stop.

Review both sets of designs. Select the three designs that appeal most to you. Tape the designs to the poster board. Display the chosen patterns somewhere in your home, like the refrigerator, bulletin board, or table top. Put the other designs in a large plastic bag and put away for later inspiration.

Creativity Exercise 2: Build a Poem

Materials

Paper, pen or pencil

Directions

Sit at a quiet table to work. The first task is to realize that you may have a fantasy about poetry, and the fantasy is getting in your way. If your fantasy is like most people's, you have the notion that poetry is supposed to be "good." Nothing could be further from reality. A lot of published poetry is not very good and your poetry doesn't have to meet anyone's standards but yours. Give up the fantasy and get on with the fun.

The second task is to read through the directions before beginning to write. Although they are presented as steps, you need to have a complete understanding of the entire task before beginning any part of it.

Poetry can take many forms—odes, sonnets, rhyming, haiku, and so on. Poetry is simply a way of expressing feelings and thoughts through words used with imagination and beauty. Thus, the most important thing is that you search for words and phrasing to express your feelings and thoughts about something. There are even kits of words and phrases on magnets that you can combine to form a poem. That would be a good sequel to this exercise.

This exercise uses image expansion to write a poem. The steps are as follows:

- Allow an image to emerge. It doesn't matter what the image is, just that it means something to you. Another way to do it is to select something in your world that has meaning and use it as the image to work with.

- Name or label the image. Try to limit the name or label to one word, two at the most.

- Using two words for one and four words for two, describe the essence of what the image does.

- Using three words for one and five words for two, tell how you feel about the image.

- Using two words for one and four words for two, describe your relationship with the image.

- Finally, using one word or two, rename the image.

Following is an example.

Image	Car
Label	Transportation
Essence	Reliable, safe,
Feelings	Cared for, protected, needed
Relationship	Pleased, concerned
Renamed	Vital

This is your poem, simple as it is. The words can be left as they are or woven into another version of a poem. Remember, I did say that the poetry did not have to be good.

The idea is that you can use the process to express feelings. And, if you use an image that has strong personal significance for you, the feelings will be stronger and easier to label, making the image expansion much more of a poem.

Creativity Exercise 3: My Favorites

Materials

Recent photo of you and one you especially like, both featuring you alone; magazines and catalogues, glue stick, large piece of white poster board, large shape of your choice for tracing (see directions for shape), large sheet of newsprint, scissors, pencil, felt-tipped marker in black, a favorite color, or metallic color

Directions

Sit at a quiet table where you won't be disturbed. Play quiet music in the background if you like. Choose one of the following as your large shape: heart, star, circle, square, rectangle, equilateral triangle, diamond, hexagon, or oval. If none of these appeal to you, select one of your choice that is simple and plain. The intent is to draw the chosen shape on the poster board in the center, with approximately one-and-a-half-inch borders at the top and bottom and two-inch borders at the sides.

Begin by drawing the shape on the newsprint. This allows you to make corrections before drawing on the poster board. When you are satisfied with the shape, cut it out and trace around it on the poster board lightly with the pencil. You will go over it with the felt marker after you complete the rest of the collage.

Place your photo in the middle of the shape and glue it. Use the magazines and catalogues to find pictures and symbols for:

- things

- people

- relationships

- activities

- accomplishments

- dreams

- hobbies

that are important to you and define you. Carefully cut them out until you have a rather large collection. Glue these in the shape, around your photo. You may want to lay them out on the shape before gluing so that you can rearrange them to please you. This is a collage so the pictures can overlap, be different sizes, and go in different directions. They don't have to be lined up in any way. When you cut out pictures, try to cut away the surrounding parts so that the item stands on its own.

When you're finished gluing, carefully trace the pencil outline with the felt-tipped marker of your choice. The final step is to give your creation a title. Print the title below the collage.

Creativity Exercise 4: Doodling Rainbow

Materials

Collect some examples of your doodles or draw a few on a piece of paper, three large sheets of newsprint, a large sheet of while artist's paper (heavier stock than newsprint), a set of colored felt-tipped markers, colored pencils, watercolor pencils, or oil pastels (select one of these), pencil

Directions

Sit at a table or stand at an easel and examine your doodles. Use the ones that have endured through the years or those that appeal most to you. The three sheets of newsprint are for practice before putting your creation on the artist's paper.

Look at the newsprint and visualize how your doodles would form a rainbow, one doodle on each band of the rainbow. Select a symbol (something like the sun) for an anchor. Draw the rays flowing from or to the anchor. Each ray will be a different color, so decide which doodle will go on which ray. The sheets of newsprint give you an opportunity to try different versions. Once you have one that is acceptable, draw it on the white artist paper.

Select a color for each ray of the rainbow. Of course your rainbow can have the color placement of your choice. Generally rainbows cluster the cool colors together (green, blue, purple), the warm colors together (yellow, orange, red), and shading from intense at the foot of the rainbow to light at the top. However you'd like to present your doodles rainbow is okay.

Be sure to step back frequently and look at your rainbow.

Creativity Exercise 5: Feelings Essays

Materials
Notebook, pen

Directions
Make sure you have a hard surface to write on and a comfortable, quiet place to sit. Each feeling will be described in a one- to two-page essay. Although five feelings are suggested here, there is no limit on the number of essays that can be written.

Feelings essays are descriptions of your feelings *as you experience them*. Be as fully descriptive as possible, using some or all of the following as guides. The five feelings suggested are love, sadness, anger, happiness, and contentment.

Guides
- **Bodily sensations**: What does the feeling produce in your body (tingling, warmth, cold)? Where is it located in your body? Does it move as you experience it (begins in chest and moves to head)?

- **Shape**: If your feeling had a shape, what would it be?

- **Size**: Is this a large, medium, small, or tiny feeling?

- **Color**: Give the feeling a color.

- **Control**: The extent of control you have over the feeling. Can you consciously initiate the feeling or does it spontaneously emerge? Can you suppress it, or does it seem to have a mind of its own?

Try and develop a phrase that capture the essence of the feeling for you. For example, "Love, the all-encompassing connectedness," "Irritation, the itch or tickle that cannot be reached." Search for descriptors by allowing your imagination to make some associations.

Don't allow yourself to get stuck by searching for the exact word or phrase. Whatever you write is not written in stone, it can be changed by you at any time.

Creativity Exercise 6: Paper Pictures

Materials

Scene from a child's coloring book or a large scene from a magazine, large sheets of tracing paper, scissors, patterned and plain origami paper or wrapping paper, glue, pencil, poster tape

Optional Materials

Mounting board, frame

Directions

Trace the outline of a scene. The coloring book was suggested because these books usually have very bold outlines that can easily be followed. If you choose to have a scene from a magazine, select one that doesn't have a lot of small details.

Use the poster tape to attach tracing paper to the scene. Lightly trace the outline of everything you want to include in the picture. You can omit some things or even include some things that you draw or find in other pictures. For example, if you want to include a butterfly in your picture, you could draw one or find one in another picture to trace.

Make two tracings of the scene. One tracing will be used as the pattern and the other as the backing for the product. Cut out the shapes from one of the tracings. Place the shapes on the back of the origami or wrapping paper and either trace around them or cut them out without tracing. Place the cut-out shapes on the other tracing and glue. Mount and frame.

Creativity Exercise 7: Easy Images

Materials

Crayons, charcoal, or a broad point drawing pencil, tracing, parchment, or vellum paper, either white or light color, mat and frame, masking tape, spray fixer

Directions

You will be making "rubbings" of several objects of various sizes. Your paper choice should be large enough to go from the top to the bottom of the object. Begin with a small object, but select one that is not too small.

Practice your rubbing with crayons or pencil, as it is very easy to smudge charcoal. Make several practice rubbings until you are satisfied with your technique.

Rubbings are very easy to do. Basically, you are rubbing a crayon or pencil over an object with raised surfaces that then appear as an outline. Be sure to select objects with raised surfaces and not too many details. Practice using: coins, a screen, a brick wall or walkway, a pendant, twigs, the tops of small boxes with designs, or anything of interest to you. Practice on a small object that is flat and easy to secure so that it does not move around as you rub. If the object tends to slide around, make a double-sided cylinder out of masking tape to hold the object still on the table.

Lightly rub the marker across the object until you're satisfied with the outline. Experiment using different colors, if you wish.

Once you make a few practice rubbings, including practicing with the charcoal, you are ready to do a final one.

Begin by noticing objects that interest you and would make good rubbings. Look for offbeat, interesting surfaces.

You do not have to use the entire object—you could limit yourself to partial details. Places and objects that have surfaces and details for rubbings include:

- graveyards with old tombstones

- molding in old buildings

- churches

- wrought-iron furniture and fences

- furniture

- cabinet doors.

Look for carvings, embossed surfaces, and the like. Some three-dimensional objects can be rubbed, but securing the object and paper can be a challenge. If you want to try rubbing a very large object, use butcher paper that comes in rolls. When you're done, spray the rubbing with the fixer so that it won't smudge.

Once you have your rubbing, mat and frame it. Display it somewhere in your world.

Creativity Box

Once you accept that you are creative, you may want to make yourself a "Creativity Box," a container for your materials and supplies for expressing your thoughts and feelings. It doesn't have to be a box, but could be a drawer, a room, a place, a basket, and so on. Keep your writing and drawing materials there so that they're readily available. This is also the place where you can collect and keep objects that can provide inspiration for your creative endeavors. Make a vow to visit your box often.

Expanding and Enhancing

Following are some suggestions for enhancing and expanding your creativity.

- Take a class to learn techniques for expressing your creativity. Classes are offered in art, music, dance, writing, flower arranging, and so on at low cost in community recreation programs, church programs, school systems' external education programs, and many college and university continuing-education programs. Try something you haven't done before.

- Buy, or borrow from the library, a book on a craft of your choice and follow the directions. Many inexpensive magazines and books are available from craft stores.

- Look in the local newspaper for "guild" or group meetings that feature creating (writing, quilting, embroidery, pottery) and attend. Not only can you learn, you will make new friends.

- Teach a craft to children. Observe how they use their creativity with the craft.

- Look at everyday items and objects and think of new uses for them.

- Find some wonder every day.

Chapter 10

Wrap-up Thoughts

One important premise of this book is that parental destructive narcissism has far-reaching consequences. These parents' behaviors and attitudes affect their children, who, in turn, can unwittingly transmit some to their children. Thus, it's important for more than personal reasons to become aware of the impact your parents' destructive narcissism had on you and any lingering aspects of underdeveloped narcissism you may have. Your personal life, relationships, and well-being are not the only things at stake. If you have children, your children and their children may also be impacted.

Remember that you don't have to remain in the same state you were as a child, when your destructive narcissistic parent:

- cared more for their needs than yours

- considered you as an extension of self

- competed with you for attention and admiration

- was unemphatic and insensitive

- demanded love and affection from you but gave little or none in return

- continually put you down and undermined your confidence

- was unable to be pleased or satisfied

- did not foster separation and individuation for you

- could not understand or relate to important and intense feelings

- expected you to attend to them and subjugate your needs and desires in favor of theirs.

It's possible to change your expectations, behaviors, and attitudes so that you do not continue to respond to the parent as you did when you were a child. You don't have to continue to experience the intensely unpleasant feelings that characterize interactions with the destructive narcissistic parent. Nor are you doomed to repeat the destructive narcissistic behaviors and attitudes in your life. Change is possible and is the best thing you could do for yourself.

You may have been somewhat overwhelmed as you read through this book. Memories and old feelings could have been triggered and found to be as fresh, intense, and unpleasant today as they were during the remembered events. Years of frustration you experienced when interacting and coping with the parent can also contribute to feeling overwhelmed. There is so much to take in, understand about the parent and about yourself, and sort out that you may not know where to start. Maybe it's all whirling around in very complex ways.

One way to find your way and get on track is through working with a competent therapist. There are many such mental- health professionals all over the world. They may have differing professional titles (counselor, psychologist, psychotherapist, clinical social worker, psychiatrist, etc.) and the choice of a therapist is individualistic. The licensing and professional organizations for each profession have materials and suggestions that can help guide your choice.

Whether you choose to work with a therapist or not, there are actions you can take that will be helpful.

- Give up your fantasy.

- Accept your inability to change the parent.

- Protect yourself.

- Engage in self-exploration and assessment.

- Develop your lingering aspects of underdeveloped narcissism.

- Understand that the parent simply cannot see the impact of their behavior and attitudes.

- Be patient.

- Expect each change you make to be small and celebrate each one.

Give Up Your Fantasy

Give yourself the wonderful gift of letting go of the unrealistic fantasies you have about your parent. This destructive narcissistic parent is not likely to become what you yearn for as a parent, perceive you and love you as you want, nor be warm, loving, and empathic. Giving up those expectations will save you a lot of heartache.

On the other hand, you can give these to yourself and others. You can parent yourself as your parent could. Take an inventory of how you never may follow your parent's example in the way you treat yourself. For example, do you put yourself down, make self-depreciating remarks, get down on yourself when you make mistakes, and so on. When you give up the fantasy that your parent will stop doing these things, you will also be able to stop doing them to yourself and begin treating yourself with the care and tenderness you yearn for from your parent.

Giving up the fantasy will not be easy since you've spent a lifetime hoping. You may find "thought stopping" to be helpful. When you find yourself thinking:

- "Why doesn't he/she _____?"

- "Why does he/she _____?"

- "If only he/she would just once _____"

- "Can't she/he see what the negative impact is on me?"

- "I want my parent to _____"

- "He/she could change if they wanted to"

stop and remind yourself that what you're asking for is a reflection of your fantasy.

Accept Your Limitations

Infants and children are appropriately grandiose. They perceive that the world revolves around them and their needs. You, as an adult, do not have the same excuse for your grandiose fantasy that you can make your parent change to suit you. You simply can't do or say anything to make them change, and it is important that you realize this and accept your limitations.

You may want to take inventory of how you try to control the attitudes and behaviors of others in your life, as this need may be a reflection of your deep-seated yearning to have your parent change. It would not be unusual to find that you are displacing this need on others as a defense against knowing that you can't change your parent.

Accepting your limitations is important to your psychological growth and development and begins with recognizing that others are:

- not extensions of you

- not under your control

- individuals who have the right to make their own decisions and establish personal values

- not obliged to do what you want them to

- capable and competent

- allowed to make mistakes

- able to care for themselves

- not appreciative of your efforts to control them.

The next time you want to tell someone what he/she should or ought to do, give advice, or think that you know what is best for someone, stop and remind yourself that you may be substituting control of that person for your lack of control over your parent. Repeat to yourself, until you believe it, that you cannot do anything to make your parent change.

Protect Yourself

One helpful action you can take is to protect yourself. Go back and reread the section on emotional insulation, as it is very important for you to be able to take steps to protect yourself from your destructive narcissistic parent's projections and projective identifications. You'll need to stop incorporating and identifying with their projections and become more aware of which feelings are yours (arising from within you) and which feelings are being projected on you (the parent's feelings). Reducing or eliminating intense, unpleasant reactions that are really your parent's projections can be of considerable help and relief.

There are other steps you can take to protect yourself such as:

- limiting interactions

- controlling the time and duration of any interaction

- changing your nonverbal behavior so that you are not physically attending to the parent

- forcing yourself to make neutral or noncommittal responses

- rigidly reinforcing your boundaries when dealing with the parent

- building and developing your psychological growth.

You have to practice whatever protective strategies you choose and institute them constantly with your parent. This means that you must increase your awareness and remind yourself to institute the strategy. Eternal vigilance is the key, and the payoff is that you will be less frustrated, angry, upset, and hurt, and will feel more in charge of yourself.

Self-Exploration and Assessment

I'd like to especially emphasize self-exploration and assessment. There are numerous exercises in this book to focus and guide readers in these directions, and you are encouraged to complete some of them. If you are really dedicated or curious, you could do all of them.

Another emphasis is personal growth, and self-exploration and assessment facilitates your understanding of where you need to grow and how to go about it. By knowing yourself better, you'll be able to develop coping strategies consistent with your personality and situation. You really need to know and understand something about the reasons you respond to your parent as you do and how you may be contributing to your own distress. Not that the parent isn't doing or saying upsetting and distressful things—he/she is. However, you are also playing a part in your distress, and learning more about yourself can help show you how you can stop doing things to aid and abet the destructively narcissistic parent.

The primary benefit for self-exploration and assessment is that your awareness and self-knowledge will be substantially increased. What you'll also find is that you will be better able to understand others. You can increase your:

- acceptance of others
- tolerance of differences
- respect for other perspectives
- ability to express important feelings
- empathy and empathic responses
- understanding of your boundaries
- confidence and self-efficacy.

Developing Your Healthy Narcissism

The ideal is to have healthy adult narcissism. But, just as your destructive narcissistic parent cannot see their underdeveloped narcissism, you may not be aware of lingering aspects of underdeveloped narcissism you may have. But you, unlike your parent, are willing to try to become more aware of those personal areas that need developing.

The scales and some exercises in this book identify some of the behaviors and attitudes that, when clustered, can be considered indicative of underdeveloped narcissism. When you examine your behavior, attitudes, feelings, and feedback from others, you can begin to identify areas that need strengthening. For example, you can specifically:

- stop doing some things

- experiment with new behaviors

- think through your reactions and decide if they are reasonable

- think instead of simply reacting

- increase behaviors that are effective.

What you do not want to do is to become depressed or overwhelmed by the need for developing your underdeveloped narcissism. It may seem daunting when you first take inventory, but even large tasks do not have to be tackled all at once. Break them down into smaller, more manageable tasks. Work on a little at a time.

It could be helpful to keep a journal or some record of your development. In it you could begin by listing your goals and objectives. A goal is an end accomplishment and objectives are steps you take to reach the goal. For example, if the goal were to reduce your need for attention, some objectives could be to:

- quietly enter and leave rooms

- become comfortable when others have the attention

- not do or say anything to "upstage" the person who has the attention

- refrain from changing topics to one that features you and your concerns

- get a trusted friend or spouse to agree to a nonverbal signal to let you know when you are boasting or bragging.

Begin with only one or two goals and keep a record of achievement toward the goals. You could list failures and relapses, but since your awareness has intensified you will probably be very aware of any failures. It may not be necessary to record them, although recording would be a very good reminder.

It could also be helpful to read your goals, objectives, and achievements often. Remind yourself of how far you have progressed toward your goal(s) and take pleasure in your achievements.

When you make satisfactory progress toward the chosen goal, it's time to select another goal and formulate objectives. Keep chipping away at understanding your lingering aspects of underdeveloped narcissism and working on your healthy narcissism. You can do both at the same time. For example, you can increase your humor, creativity, and empathic responses. Review the chapters on these topics for suggestions on behaviors that can be target goals. Practice nonverbal and verbal empathic responding in all aspects of your life and with almost everyone. "Almost" is used because there may be people in your world with whom it is dangerous to be empathic. Above all, do not try to be empathic with your destructive narcissistic parent. It did not work before, and it will not work now.

Understand Your Parent

You probably better understand some of your parent's behaviors and attitudes after reading this book. On some level, understanding helps you cope, but this person can undoubtably still arouse frustration, hurt, anger, and exasperation.

The common fantasy is that the parent is very much aware of the impact on you and is deliberately ignoring your anguish. The reality is that they do not see the impact and when you try to explain it to the parent, your responses are devalued or minimized, leading to more frustration.

In order for the parent to be in touch with the negative impact on you, he/she would have to be aware of and admit that he/she was flawed in some way. That bit of information is not available to their conscious understanding and the person who even suggests such is perceived as trying to hurt or destroy them. The parent's very strong defenses are mounted, both against knowing and against the threatening person. Thus, in a nanosecond, any hint that the parent is flawed is submerged or destroyed.

You must constantly remind yourself of your parent's inability to see the impact of his/her behavior and attitudes on you. Every time you react negatively to a comment or attitude, stop and say to yourself that the parent is simply unaware of what they are doing and its impact. In addition, refrain from trying to make them more aware by:

- crying
- screaming
- verbally rebuking the parent
- telling the parent off
- retaliating with a put-down or sarcastic remark
- telling the parent the impact on you
- pointing out the parent's flaws and failings.

These will not work with your parent and may have the unintended effect of making you feel worse.

Be Patient with Yourself

You may want to have everything turn around at once. This is called "magical thinking." If it were possible to wave a magic wand and immediately effect change, things would be simpler, but no magic wands are available. Just hard work, some pain, and slow progress. There may even be some failures and setbacks along the way.

However, if you mobilize your inner resources and strengths, be persistent and determined, not become discouraged by momentary failures, and continue to develop your healthy narcissism, you can succeed. Progress may be slow, but it can also be steady.

Be patient, especially with yourself. It has taken quite some time to become who you are; and it will take time to effect changes. Do not fall into the trap of getting down on yourself because you make mistakes or don't change fast enough. Remember to take time to look at the positive changes you are able to make and not always stay acutely in touch with your failures.

When you slip, fail, or it seems as if no progress is being made, take an inventory of how you can improve your progress. For example, if your destructive narcissistic parent once again got under your skin after you vowed not to get angry, replay the situation to see where you could make future changes. It could be that you forgot your emotional insulation, tried to confront, or engaged in a self-defeating behavior. Instead of getting down on yourself for getting upset, use that energy to make positive changes.

Celebrate Your Progress

Allow yourself to celebrate changes and progress. Do not take them for granted. You may have had to endure some real pain with your self-examination and much hard work to effect changes. These are not minor, and you must take steps not to minimize them. Others are only too willing to do that for you.

Celebration does not mean a party or other public event. What I mean by "celebration" could be:

- a quiet, inner flush of pleasure
- a personal pat on the back
- dancing around by yourself saying, "Yes!"
- throwing your arms up to signal a "touchdown"
- a visualization of you receiving applause
- smiling at yourself in the mirror
- putting a "bounce" in your walk.

When you celebrate, be sure to reward yourself in some small way. Some of the ways I reward myself are:

- a new mystery book
- indulging in a new craft
- trying new makeup or nail color

- a taste treat
- a bottle of wine more expensive than usual
- shopping with my daughters
- a trip to the museum or art gallery.

Final Words

If you are the adult child of a parent, or parents, who have a destructive narcissistic pattern, you probably feel that life has handed you a lemon. The old response to being handed a lemon is to "make lemonade." However, that response is simply not as expansive and creative as it could be.

A cartoon I love shows how limiting "making lemonade" is. The first panel shows a man in a therapist's office who is told that life has certainly handed him a lemon. The second panel shows the man thinking. The third panel shows the therapist asking the man if he'd decided how he could "make lemonade." The man responds that, actually, he thought he would buy lemon futures and set up a franchise for lemonade stands. That cartoon started me thinking about other ways to use that lemon, such as:

- scraping the rind for lemon zest and selling it
- planting seeds, starting a lemon grove, and selling the plants for ornamental gardens
- making lemon cookies and selling them or giving them to charitable organizations that feed people
- using lemons as models for still-life paintings or photographs
- starting an Internet business selling lemon zest and cookies
- drying the rinds, putting them in net bags, and using them as car, closet, and drawer fresheners
- securing research and development funds to find new uses for lemons, just as George Washington Carver did for peanuts.

Join me and expand the list.

The basic point is that you are not forever limited by the actions and non-actions of your destructive narcissistic parent. You have the potential to develop and grow in ways you cannot envision at this time. You can begin by making small changes and becoming comfortable with unleashing your imagination and creativity to help plot your direction. Building healthy adult narcissism will be the foundation for expanding and enhancing your potential, for doing so is the basis for:

- having strong and meaningful relationships that are satisfying and endure

- connecting us to others and allowing them to connect with us

- securing purpose and meaning for our lives that is by choice and not by imposition

- building safe, secure boundaries that define where we end and others begin

- understanding how freedom and responsibility are intertwined

- giving up unproductive and unrealistic expectations and yearnings

- having a sense of confidence about our abilities, competencies, and efficacy

- gaining an ability to reach out to others that helps them and does not enmesh us

- the strong realization that we cannot change others nor have the right to demand that they change to suit us.

I wish you much success and know that, with some effort, you will reach your goals.

References

Baszormenyi-Nagy, I., and J. L. Framo. 1985. *Intensive Family Therapy*. New York: Brunner/Mazel.

Brown, N. 1998. *The Destructive Narcissistic Pattern*. Westport, Conn.: Praeger.

Hafen, B. Q., K. K. Karren, K. J. Frandsen, and N. L. Smith. 1996. *Mind/Body Health*. Boston: Allyn & Bacon.

Karpel, M. A., and E. S. Strauss. 1983. *Family Evaluation*. New York: Gardner Press.

Korzybski, A. 1958. *Science and Sanity: An Introduction to Aristotelian Systems and General Semantics. 4th ed*. Lakeville, Conn.: International Non-Aristoletian Library Publishing Co.

Kohut, H. 1977. *The Restoration of the Self*. New York: International Universities Press.

Minuchin, S. 1974. *Families and Family Therapy*. Cambridge: Harvard University Press.

O'Neil, M. S., and C. E. Newbolt. 1994. *Boundary Power*. Antioch Tenn.: Sonlight Publishing Inc.

Reich, W. 1972. *Character Analysis*. New York: Simon & Schuster.

Some Other
New Harbinger Titles

Freeing the Angry Mind, Item 4380 $14.95

Living Beyond Your Pain, Item 4097 $19.95

Transforming Anxiety, Item 4445 $12.95

Integrative Treatment for Borderline Personality Disorder, Item 4461 $24.95

Depressed and Anxious, Item 3635 $19.95

Is He Depressed or What?, Item 4240 $15.95

Cognitive Therapy for Obsessive-Compulsive Disorder, Item 4291 $39.95

Child and Adolescent Psychopharmacology Made Simple, Item 4356 $14.95

ACT* on Life Not on Anger, Item 4402 $14.95

Overcoming Medical Phobias, Item 3872 $14.95

Acceptance & Commitment Therapy for Anxiety Disorders, Item 4275 $58.95

The OCD Workbook, Item 4224 $19.95

Neural Path Therapy, Item 4267 $14.95

Overcoming Obsessive Thoughts, Item 3813 $14.95

The Interpersonal Solution to Depression, Item 4186 $19.95

Get Out of Your Mind & Into Your Life, Item 4259 $19.95

Dialectical Behavior Therapy in Private Practice, Item 4208 $54.95

The Anxiety & Phobia Workbook, 4th edition, Item 4135 $19.95

Loving Someone with OCD, Item 3295 $15.95

Overcoming Animal & Insect Phobias, Item 3880 $12.95

Overcoming Compulsive Washing, Item 4054 $14.95

Angry All the Time, Item 3929 $13.95

Handbook of Clinical Psychopharmacology for Therapists, 4th edition, Item 3996 $55.95

Writing For Emotional Balance, Item 3821 $14.95

Surviving Your Borderline Parent, Item 3287 $14.95

When Anger Hurts, 2nd edition, Item 3449 $16.95

Calming Your Anxious Mind, Item 3384 $12.95

Ending the Depression Cycle, Item 3333 $17.95

Call **toll free, 1-800-748-6273,** or log on to our online bookstore at **www.newharbinger.com** to order. Have your Visa or Mastercard number ready. Or send a check for the titles you want to New Harbinger Publications, Inc., 5674 Shattuck Ave., Oakland, CA 94609. Include $4.50 for the first book and 75¢ for each additional book, to cover shipping and handling. (California residents please include appropriate sales tax.) Allow two to five weeks for delivery.

Prices subject to change without notice.